MIRACLE SONGS FOR THE MILLENNIUM

other books by the author

POETRY
Dawn Visions
Burnt Heart/Ode to the War Dead
This Body of Black Light Gone Through the Diamond
The Desert is the Only Way Out
The Chronicles of Akhira
The Blind Beekeeper
Mars & Beyond
Laughing Buddha Weeping Sufi
Salt Prayers
Ramadan Sonnets
Psalms for the Brokenhearted
I Imagine a Lion
Coattails of the Saint
Abdallah Jones and the Disappearing-Dust Caper (illustrated by the author)
Love is a Letter Burning in a High Wind
The Flame of Transformation Turns to Light
Underwater Galaxies
The Music Space
Cooked Oranges
Through Rose Colored Glasses
Like When You Wave at a Train and the Train Hoots Back at You
In the Realm of Neither
The Fire Eater's Lunchbreak
Millennial Prognostications
You Open a Door and it's a Starry Night
Where Death Goes
Shaking the Quicksilver Pool
The Perfect Orchestra
Sparrow on the Prophet's Tomb
A Maddening Disregard for the Passage of Time
Stretched Out on Amethysts
Invention of the Wheel
Sparks Off the Main Strike
Chants for the Beauty Feast
In Constant Incandescence
Holiday from the Perfect Crime
The Caged Bear Spies the Angel
The Puzzle
Ramadan is Burnished Sunlight
Ala-udeen & The Magic Lamp (illustrated by the author)
The Crown of Creation (illustrated by the author)
Blood Songs
Down at the Deep End (with drawings by the author)
Next Life
A Hundred Little 3D Pictures
He Comes Running (chapbook)
Miracle Songs for the Millennium

THEATER / THE FLOATING LOTUS MAGIC OPERA COMPANY
The Walls Are Running Blood
Bliss Apocalypse

PROSE
Zen Rock Gardening
The Little Book of Zen

MIRACLE SONGS FOR THE MILLENNIUM

poems

January 23 - October 16, 1996

Daniel Abdal-Hayy Moore

The Ecstatic Exchange
2014
Philadelphia

Miracle Songs for the Millennium
Copyright © 2014 Daniel Abdal-Hayy Moore
All rights reserved.
Printed in the United States of America

For quotes any longer than those for critical articles and reviews, contact:
The Ecstatic Exchange,
6470 Morris Park Road, Philadelphia, PA 19151-2403
email: abdalhayy@danielmoorepoetry.com

First Edition
ISBN: 978-0-578-13831-2 (paper)
Published by *The Ecstatic Exchange,*
6470 Morris Park Road, Philadelphia, PA 19151-2403

Also available from *The Ecstatic Exchange:*
Knocking from Inside, poems by Tiel Aisha Ansari

Cover collage, back photo and book design by the author

DEDICATION

To
Shaykh ibn al-Habib
(and the continuation of the Habibiyya)
Shaykh Bawa Muhaiyuddeen,
all shuyukh of instruction and ma'arifa
and
Baji Tayyaba Khanum
of the unsounded depths

✼

*The earth is not bereft
of Light*

TABLE OF CONTENTS

Returning from a Marvelous Journey   11
Put Ladders Up Against the Sky Everywhere   13
Drunken Aphorisms   16
The Treasury of the Sky   19
I Scent My Beard Before I Sleep   20
I Look Through My Eyes   23
Microscopic Twigs   25
Other-Dimensional Latitudes   28
In the Courtyard of the Prophets   30
God's Echo   32
Snail   34
Multi-Colored Skies   36
Sunflower of Fortune   38
Configurations of Sleepers   42
Stethoscope   43
The Well   45
Shadow on the Moon   47
Reply to a Letter from a Long-Lost Friend   50
In the Tiniest Mirror   53
Orchestrated by Angels   55
The Sky is Red   58
It's a Different Location   59
Dawn Prayer   62
Cat   64
Blizzard Bacchanal   66
At the Command of the Sky   68
Ember Falling Through Space   69
Mind Piano   72

God's in the Details   76
Watching People Pass By   79
Angels Sing   82
Journey   84
The World   86
Nude, I Bear You   87
Hands to the Sides of our Heads   89
Nature Poetry   95
Maybe Nobody's Really Happy   97
When Someone   100
Contemplation on the Rocks   101
First-hand Sunlight, First-hand Rock   105
We Have Come a Long Way   107
A Version of Petrarch   109
Trees, For All Their Beauty   110
A New Stone   113
Wrong Side of the Bed   114
Dawn Song   116
Answered Prayer   118
First One Angel   121
Baby Dawn Blue   123
The Alchemist's Lapse   124
On This Side of Sleep   128
Possible Angels   131
Advice in our Sleep   133
Ruby Red   134
Behind Every Patch of Sunlight   137
Résumé   141
Mother Tongue   146
I Spy a Land Beyond Clouds   149
One of Us   151

Song for the Millennium   153
From Where I Sit   155
Little Black Fly on the Wall   156
I Don't Know   158
In This World of Multiple Solitaries   160
Greenness of My Garden   162
Out in the Longitudinal Air   163
It's Hard if You're Dead   165
I End My Song   169
Tom-Tom   171
Keeping Watch   174
Everything Was as it Should Be   176
Upward Shower of Pure Sound   178
Fables Written During a Flight from Chicago to Philadelphia   180
The Rain Has Been Falling   184
New York   186
I Wake Up with a Start   188
Pythian the Angler   189
King of Locusts   191
Eyelash   193
The Bee   195
Light   197
Cricket   200
Water Running in the Pipes   202
All Your Messages   203
Some Sleep!   206
The Ear That Hears It   208
Funeral Practices   210
Rain   214
Big Boat of the Night   217
The Soul   218

Straight on Ahead Through Green   220
Notebook   222
Passing a Crushed Squirrel on the Highway   226
Ocean   227
What He'll Have to Learn   229

INDEX   232

The setting in order of strewn beads is the same as the setting in order of scattered words, which is poetry; its coming into being is the net of the hunter. Only that which has life (spirit) is caught in the net, and speech and poetry have no life except they are of God.

— Ibn ʿArabi (Sufis of Andalusia)

RETURNING FROM A MARVELOUS JOURNEY

I've got a window up my sleeve
   and a door in my shirt
I can open any time to walk
   out into the blue. Arch my
     arm and see
meadows, sunbursts, vistas.
Pantaloons of mileage, shoes of market silver,
windy hair from lunar rocky mountaintops
   shagging this way and that
like a semaphore signaling which
   road to come in on, which
circuitous loop to take to the
      interior.

All this from being in the Land of Marvelous Vision,
Place of Collapsing Mirrors,
the spiral staircase from heaven to earth
down which, in diaphanous gowns of mist,
come tall ladies of supernatural beauty
with cats' eyes and lips of lapis lazuli.

I saw a blind man pick up a crystal
   and see through it to the
      ends of the earth.

I saw a protean bird change shape a
   hundred times and end up a
     small boy with red shovel

      standing in sand.

My beloved's eyes put a second moon in orbit,
my beloved's lips send shivers across Jupiter's hills,

my beloved's heartbeats drumming rhythms in
Pluto's clouds balance on sharp mountaintops before
   scudding off into

shadowy territories.

PUT LADDERS UP AGAINST THE SKY EVERYWHERE

Put ladders up against the sky everywhere —
I'm climbing to the stars!

Why else did God create us? Not to
   mope among brick walls.

Throw your glass against the door of love and
   let its hinges groan!

No sleeper moves from his place, no
   dead man finishes his nap and
     gets up and puts on socks.

The rush of birds past the window can
   never be reversed.

The gray hair hanging long on either side of
   Dame Age's lusterless cheeks
is not about to enjoy Spring again,
    flowers peeping their
      bright purple faces between
        strands.

If you have to paint your horse blue,
    do it!
If that's what it takes to open the rock doors
   of your heart while the

    west wind is blowing
then let no minute drag its fishnets to
    shore with less than
ten tons of fish, and they should
    all be smiling and
        calling out their names to us
to remember them in our prayers before they
    stare-eyed, silently sink into death.

I've been circling around the subject all my life
like an inebriate, or an Alzheimer's patient
    who's forgotten which door he needs to
        take to go to bed.

Bees buzz and flies buzz, but how different
    their goal and their sanctity!
One brown-noses garbage and washes its
    hands and legs on a
        dunghill.
The other gathers pollen and
  fuzzes the flowers one after another
    until the sun goes down.
One produces grubs, the other honey.

I would sing in the bee choir on High
    Holy days, hang with the
bees around the lilac tavern,
    drunk on nectar!

What's fame to someone who's lost nothing but
space and time before the

oncoming locomotive runs us down?
Clouds surround us, carry us off into
    territories of mist.

Oh God, did I say I missed you?

Did I say that the flower wilted in my lapel
has been whispering Your Name?

                                                  1/23

DRUNKEN APHORISMS

Before the life train slows down
   throw yourself in front of it.

Is it made of roses, is it made of love?

You can't bottle vinegar and
   sell it as wine.

You can't lie like a corpse and be
   invited to the party.

Go to the Kaaba and
   throw yourself in front of it.

If your name is called
   remember you're a slave.

Put the glass crown aside
   and wear the cap of shame.

Leave your shoes at the door, and your
   jacket with the medals.

Unzip your skin and stride free
   into sunlight.

As day progresses the fiendish wearers of masks
   grow drowsy.

Noisemakers grow faint under the
    low hum of commerce.

Bridge-makers have erected superstructures
    and systems.

For a while we suppose it's safe
    to come out.

Safe to cross bridges into enemy territory.
Safe to go shopping among demons and
    hornéd beasts.

Safe to put hard-earned money
    down on countertops of flame.

But if we've traded hearts of light for
    idols made of beeswax
nothing can save us now
except pain and sorrow's blight.

Then distant doors rattle and
    windows chime with birdsong,

smoke leaves the room
and miraculous crystals appear.

I can see as far as China when I
    listen to heartsong.

I can see as far as my fingertips when

I fall into sleep.

China's an immense ruby
    poised over an abyss.

People say *"Good morning"* with
    doves in their pockets.

Words hang in air like
balloons made of tissue paper.

"Seek knowledge as far as China"
and you'll come back speaking English.

Ink stains fingertips of
someone who's fished for squid.

Dare not, taste not! O

throw yourself down. How can you
distinguish between true
    words and a groan?

God, You called me to sit up after dawn,
hold my pen in my hand and
    write.

Don't abandon me to my imagination
if You don't fill it full of Light!

                                                         1/23

THE TREASURY OF THE SKY

Now the sky's blue, now it's red with thunder.
Now it's full of angels, now it's blank as paste.

Now the sky's enlarging, expanding to the stars.
Now the sky's as small as a pin-prick in a
    finger poised in witness.

I've never seen it open its doors, yet
   know they exist in it somewhere.

I've heard the sounds of its distant furniture
   scraping across cloud's floors.

Things stand up and come forth in it.
Things lie down in it and die.

We've all got a major investment
   in the treasury of the sky.

                                                     1/23

I SCENT MY BEARD BEFORE I SLEEP

I scent my beard before I sleep to
   please the angels.

How many tabletops across this earth
   have a layer of salt
      instead of a layer of starlight
upon which they set down their glasses of
      crystal nectar?

I see green hills in the distance
   dotted with white horses with
      golden wings.

Now the black sky fills with round clouds.

Sun-slant comes beaming down and they
   browse in and out of
      spotlights of gold the
   beams make on the grass.

Some of the horses have human faces, some are
   my friends from childhood, some of
      people I've never met but who
did *tawaf* of the Kaaba in Mecca when I was there
and now stand in eternity on a green hillside
with soft eyes and
softly closing wings.

What's to become of my daily life, if it's not

drenched with these visions?

I fear I might yell at the grocery clerk
   for seeming to forget that
at his back or her back
a screen of closely woven butterfly dust
opens onto an ocean we can walk
   out on without fear of
      drowning.

The passport to the other side is even more
insubstantial than dreams
but more capable of supporting our
   daily weight with all its
     bewildering fluctuations.

The little white horses blink.

When their eyelashes sweep down
   the world darkens.
When they sweep up
   you meet a stranger and
     exchange a meaningful
       glance, openly, of love.

The sound now of small hooves on glass cobblestones.

The sound of celestial singing deep in their
     throats.

I knew I'd seen them before

around the Kaaba.
And I knew I'd see them again, O God,
on Your round earth!

Give them my deepest love, and let the
   tips of their wings
      tremble in the light. For this

love dissipates darkness. It's like a

door opened up in a mountainside

to let us enter.

But to enter it is to enter Paradise.

And the sun hasn't set yet

on this world.

                                              1/24

I LOOK THROUGH MY EYES

I look through my eyes and see my own
   eyes looking out.
I close my eyes tightly and a solar redness appears
in front of pervasive darkness.
The world is wedged inside my head with perfect fit
   the way the nerves of my arms
      run along my arms.
I move freely in three dimensions
and the air all around me is like a
   silent slow-motion waterfall.
     People pass
into and out of it. They do not sit
next to me as I write this.

If I threw all terminology away and resorted only to
signs to make myself understood,
or juggled bottles, or ate fire,
or walked on miniature pyramids of
   live coals, or rode
elevators up and down fifty-story buildings all day
to disperse this sense of anatomical confinement,
then perhaps I'd experience a vast sky full of
migratory birds, or
horizons where giant schooners appear then
   disappear into the Bermuda Triangle,
or who-knows-what,
the universe turned inside-out so I could
   survey the newly discovered

billion or so million-year-old galaxies lying
   just off starboard —

but, in fact, this bodily cage is our lot here on earth,
it goes with being an earthling among other
   earthlings, it is
     miracle enough in
shoes and socks and filled trousers and shirts
as well as feet and knees and
well-tailored arms and breasts of being
   human, through which we experience
God's ineffably numinous manifestations in
     constant flux,
  rainbows spouting out at surprising latitudes
   and odd angles,
people speaking the most amazing
   unscripted dialog at
understandable intervals with each other,
the whole tropical and sub-tropical and
temperate biomass of

eyes to look out of, fingers to touch with,
hearts full of candlelit processions
to the main arena, where
harmonious voices in
pure white robes with silver hoods

explain the details of the universe
in thousand-part harmony so
aligned with the angels as to be
virtually indistinguishable.

                                          1/25

MICROSCOPIC TWIGS

Pound for pound and ounce for ounce,
is this world worth little more than a
   bamboo ladder thrown up against a
      passing train?

Its flags are silk, embroidered in beauty, they
   flap in the breeze like seductive smiles,
they catch the sun and fling their
   ripples like flamenco dancers, but they're
held by toads on black lilypads in
      perpetual moonlight.

Just when the world seems to relax around its
hinges, when perpetual summer slides by like
perpetual solace, hands dipped in
   pool water,
a nasty rip appears in the fabric,
neo-Nazis in tight T-shirts
lumber in, white, white legs cutting forward from
   the cuffs of cutoffs, intellectual
distortion and factual innacuracies abound,
thought is drained away, replaced by horizons of
   kneejerk reactions,
everything one held dear is being sold at the
   Flea Market with a bar of soap,
the President promises four more years of
   secretive ineptitudes and sinister agendas,
rats are described as handsome Clark Gables,

mothers stuff babies into
   milk bottles and throw them in the sea,
the whole mechanism vibrates like an electronic
    skeleton remover
and no one can stay still for a second as the
shrill factory whistle hurls its screams into
   night like a murderer, or the
sudden screeching to a stop of our pulse-rate
or a telephone call to a drowning magistrate.

True justice always seems to be happening
  among happy villagers on
    faraway islands,
true music played by an ancient aborigine on
two thighbones and a hollow tube,
true light embraced in the heart of the
   first man and woman on earth, or the
last,

true enlightenment seems to last forever
in a mile-wide band of galactic scintillation
punctuated only by aurora borealises and rainbows
   against a black backdrop

as this tiny world bursts like a seltzer bubble
and disappears for good,
as the living saint closes his lips and opens his
eyes and opens the fingers of his
two hands
and constitutions and documents and
   secret legends of this world

drift to the ground as dry leaves

spelling apocalyptic sentences
with microscopic twigs.

1/28

OTHER-DIMENSIONAL LATITUDES

There's no getting around the terrible
   shock of reality, the inescapable
confrontation from our genetic structure
     outward
with all the consciousness and
   matter in the universe, like
billions of little stars on rafts going
in a constant flow upstream
in the very four-dimensionality of our
   existence every moment of our day,
of our waking day —
and in the great dark underground of our
    sleep where time is
elongated or compressed,
in every moment there as well, in an
    eternal spell, hypnotised by
The Enormous Presence.

As if we are wide awake in canyons.
Walls go up all around us.
They are unscaleable. Slippery. Covered with
   spiky lichens.
But straight up above is a
thin ribbon of pelucid turquoise sky.
Coolness falls from it.
Light radiates along the canyon walls.
  Almost writes messages in the
earth-ribs of the rocks.

But at the center of this constant trauma
is a Throne of Glory, supported by
   giant wings, and from that
center comes all the robust
  energies of love that irradiate the
    universe in every
instance, from gnat mothers to whale mothers
naturally solicitous of their young, tucking them
   around the mouth with
     flipper or feeler, nudging them
   on, into the
sea of this great trauma.

But I pity those who block out that
light and deny its potency,
who turn like a black corkscrew
  against its sweet delights,
who hammer on iron plates and
pound the rivets of entrapment
deeper into the bulk of death.

We savor the authoritative glance.
One who knows the Truth comes into the
sad casino and turns
   all the tables upside-down, revealing their

winged stepladders into
other-dimensional latitudes.

IN THE COURTYARD OF THE PROPHETS

In the courtyard of the prophets
  each caged canary sings such music that
the spheres join in
   in trillion-part harmony
with tree boughs drumming in the sky.

Stars sing the bass-notes.

Space itself is clear as a bell
and keeps the melody sprightly.

The prophets cast no shadows as they
   cross the polished tiles.
Their words echo long after they've spoken.
Their words ignite fiery crowns in treetops
   and make jewels of vanishing colors
     balance on the
    canaries' golden beaks.

Whether we know it or not, Malaysian
   pirates on the high seas, Mongolian
    merchants in Himalayan tea houses,
homeless in overcoats on steam-grates
   in downtown Philadelphia,
we all speak words the prophets spoke
brought down in stages from
heights of unscalable heavens, heights
  prophets know first-hand
with light splashing their faces,

opening chambers of unspeakable splendors,
    mountain ranges of glittering
blue snowlight radiating magnificently
    in their hearts.

The words are promulgated. The messages
   disseminated among molecular flakes,

we wake up with their sound caressing our
   cheeks and eyelids,

we sing their phrases in the unlocking of our
   vocal chords.

In the courtyard of the prophets
each peacock wears the face of a lawgiver,
each swallow wears a poet's swiftness
   inside each scissoring wing.

Each prophet faces another, and each
   other's face disappears in the
face of such exquisite humanity.

In the courtyard of the prophets
only One Face appears.

There is no Other.

                                                         2/5

GOD'S ECHO

I push my face through to the
   other side of the sky

into a place of no wind and no
   molecular dimension

and a horse of white light doesn't
   gallop by
flashing sparkles of purest silver in the air

and there are thin streams of water falling
   everywhere

and my eyes are as wide open as
   vowels in angelic choirs

and there is no self to stop the visions at the
   barricade of interpretation,

what will I see?

What sheets of misty sensation will pull past my
face as I blink once or twice at the
   exact rate of heartbeats
and gaze long at what I see there?

Will green valleys open up?

Will the sky and earth become
fused? Does a footstep here
   leave a footprint there
and a motion forward here
     bring about lightning-quick momentum
on distant roads? And will the

faces I meet be those of full moons wobbling
   forward in the dark, or
blessed radiances with human features
with equally open eyes and
   mouths that make
     vowels and consonants as
   naturally as
water falling, tinkling briefly on
   rocks of streams before
 joining the greatest ocean of all,

that surrounds and contains us,
but that we also contain as
cylinder within cylinder and
sphere within sphere —

the Ocean of Silence.

God's echo lying on the
   face of those waters.

2/6

SNAIL

"I had one more thing to say," he said,
   as he slid out of view.
He was consumed by ambition to become
   a snail ascending a rhododendron
      in full bloom.

His natural humility chose, for him,
   the humblest of creatures, the lowly,
homely, pea-green snail leaving its
   glistening trail of pure slime behind him
down whatever dark path under moonglow

he might slide along.

Why would one part of God's creation
be lesser or worse than another? Snail
   lesser than world leader,
      aphid rather than superstar?
Ant baby just learning to crawl, looking out its
multi-faceted eyes at a world
infinitely linear along floor, up wall,
   along ceiling and down
twig into under-loam of rich deep sweetness
   among fresh grass and
      aromatic
    decomposition.

Each twitch and wiggle of life

further proof of the
sheer delirium of God's greatness!

How many perfect snowflakes does it take to fill
a thimble full of tears?

Rivers overflow, walkways run with
   mini-oceans.

After rain, snails are happiest.
They slide along fresh moisture
   lapping it up.

"I had one more thing to say," he said,
as he slid out of view.

2/8

MULTI-COLORED SKIES

Bless us all, and forgive all of us, God, and
   let our hair hang long and green
     as grass is, and let our
bodies become pure as Spring is with its
     new sprouts, as
innocently cleansed by the raw winter of death
   and suspended animation,

let us bloom from the central rose arbors of our
   selves, deep in aroma-soaked shade,
black shadows so rich and velvety dark
out of which a single red rose opens and its
   petals transform into a
     hinged latticework of infinite
      unfoldings like
   membranous shutters expanding through the sky,

so that our
poor hearts, O God, become suitable vehicles
for whatever portion of Your Grace You may
   wish to pour,
like channels of rose-water, runnels and
arteries of sprinkler-like
     light energies
transforming this universe from a bleak orbiting chunk
held by magnetic hypnotism to the sun
to a transparent walk-up stairway through
   stars and galaxies and

    multi-colored skies
where the singing is so
    intense it's actually
       serene, sinks
imperceptibly onto our tongues,
licks the corners of our mouths of
mortals loved and forgiven by You and

aware of Your Glory!

Your Power is the sun of the universe
we adhere to.

Your Name is the galactic
center our hearts revere.

                                                  2/9

SUNFLOWER OF FORTUNE

I could face the sunflower of fortune
   and outshine its petals.
I could wear the Niagara Falls as a necklace
    around my neck.
You've awakened me with a kiss, velvety
   lips on earlobes and chin,
eyelids and deep expectation,
and I rush off on the wrong horse in the
right direction to meet you in a
daylight both of us can endure, having
sealed our vows at midnight in a
purple century long after
    midnights have any meaning
except to death's-head moths, grasshoppers and
   retired violinists who still
     play in their imaginations to
      crowded halls.

The hill is aburst with incandescent bloom,
small ivy and long tendrils looking for a
   handhold on a
    steep slope.

The light is fierce out here
among icebergs, amidst the
  barking of seals and the
shadows of a solitary polar bear
loping along in oblong sunlight.

The world has a way of flickering away in
   drops behind us the way
a polar bear shakes itself off after an
    arctic dip in pools fifty below.

Perhaps I don't exaggerate enough.

Perhaps the reality of things,
(halos around horses asleep on their feet
   in blackened fields,
the intelligence of damselfly or
    red-tailed dragonfly)
is far more extreme than any of us can
conceive, much less describe on the
    tips of our tongues, like
      torches doused in
        tombs.

Life is more hallowed, more
   sacred, more still, more
true to life than any
representation. It can be
   alluded to at the side
like the glance of an elephant, one eye
on one side of its head, or a single-sided
    whale's loving gaze underwater
as it glides past our awkward strokes in
    contraptions of complicated gear.

Measure God with His true measure —

Drop our instruments in
    awe at that
        Majesty!

The words, the sights, the
    sounds always
escape us,
all sense an escapee
before the perfection of that
    Light
running along a main highway in
    anonymous clothes,
jabbering incomprehensibly to the
first passerby who happens upon us.

We're talking fountains, canyons,
    fabulous beasts.
He sees
  dementia and
    calls the police.
We're talking deep conversations with The Divine
    in a water drop, reflections of the
Holy Face in a hubcap, or the
    muscles of mountain lions
      lying in the sun.

Our words drift like factory smoke above their
ruined cities.

Our imagery hangs like tattered washing
    outside our lives.

We're talking radiance glimpsed over a
   landscape at dawn,
     a voice from a cloud, from a
        faucet in the depths of
night.

We're talking deep conversations with
silence, the embrace of death so
   alive the insides of our
eyelids light up.

They see another casualty of mental absorption
with an unattainable ideal.

We're talking happiness with
little more than a ray of light.

We're happy

left alone in the world

whispering Your Name.

                                                    2/17

CONFIGURATIONS OF SLEEPERS

There are a thousand sleepers sleeping on a
    hillside, each one
configured differently, hands and legs and
faces arranged in the unconscious
    flamboyance of sleep.

The hillside is dark and each sleeper gives off
    an incandescent glow.
There's the World Court judge, his
    body stiff and under control.
There's the rock'n'roll superstar, heels nearly
    touching the back of his head.
Or maybe I've got it backwards.
That's the judge, the
superstar's still and stiff.

There's a child with cancer, a
    bush of tiny angels
        grown up around him.
There's the compassionate woman in white,
her cheek cradled in her palm.

A soft wind is blowing.
Each sleeper is swept along.

The mountain itself is moving
bathed in the darkness of song.

2/17

STETHOSCOPE

I recently bought a stethoscope to listen to
   any irregularities of my heart on the
     journey to Mecca,
and forgot it was there,
but months later back in my bed
I started listening to my heart and other parts of
   my body as well.

The heart's a muffled downbeat, thump and then
   a lower loop into depths unknown, then
another downbeat, deep in a cave, entering a
     mysterious space,

then the stomach and lower abdomen like
squealing little people swimming through
     tubes and speaking in
high-pitched chipmunk voices, then,
   daring the unknown even further, I put the

stethoscope satellite dish on the
   top of my head, and
     what a wonder!
A heavy rumble, continuous, ferocious,
   volcanic, a low hum of
constant activity, with sudden
   scraping sounds as of
     shingles pulled along shingles,
and I wondered if I'd breached a

   taboo here, listening with my
brain to my own brain listening,
a shudder of awesomeness, then

tried my knees, a few watery squiggles,
my sex, no sound at all, no doubt napping,
then my heart again and
couldn't quite find it, and wondered if I could hear
meadows in my feet, prostrations in echoing
   mosques in Morocco or Mecca in my
     knees, the music of the spheres
squeezed by glands and intestinal tubing, shot through with
   electric snazzle of nerve impulses, all of it
coordinated with the deftest subtlety,

finally the ear pieces making my ears sore,
the Narcissus concert
   over for the night,
the pools and lagoons of my active interior
   dropped back into shades of the

body's impenetrable darkness at last.

                                                  2/20

THE WELL

He calls down into a well
  and voices respond.

He speaks up into clouds
  and harp strings sound.

He forces his face into the blue
  and a chord resonates.

He talks directly into the earth
and echoes multiply, linked
    deep underground with
      lakes of quicksilver whose
    single touch shivers light upon light
      so bright it
        blinds.

This is pure singing.

Larks take notice, deep-sea
  carp rejoice.
Insects in the air do polkas and
  polka dots around
shafts of sound in polka downbeat
from his clicking tongue and
    happy cheeks.

He
detaches himself from the crowd.

Detaches himself from heart strings
   around the luggage of Paradise

that keeps us from Paradise.

He cuts those strings and
watches the baggage go.

Never a moment of remorse.

Never a dull thought. Each one
   a victory of ecstatic
thinking. His

heart flapping its wings,
flying between canyon rims.

Only the pure sky is his
   sure domain. Only
 secure in the
    insecure air.

His voice catching the rays.

                              2/22

SHADOW ON THE MOON

for Nur Chelsvig

I wanted to sing a song of how utterly
   vulnerable we all are.
We take one step and pull it back
  for fear the train will slice it off as it
    passes, for fear
the shoe's the wrong color, or it'll be in the
   way of the buffalo stampede,
or someone will snicker.

The railer inside doesn't think anything we do is
   wise, or good, or true.
We love and it freaks, yelling obscenities into the
   echo-stream of our love-words, so
    each one's obscene.
When we get near a window it whispers: *"Jump!"*
When we extend our shadow a fraction of a
   millisecond, it yells: *"Pride!"*
The ranting doubter, the inner pig,
   the inner traffic cop who
    issues tickets!
Well, let his siren scream!
Our resiliance is greater, our strange human
   coefficient of humble grandeur.
Our souls like personages of paper held up in a
   high wind.

Our souls like lakes of butter under a
   golden sun.
Our souls like a lick of sweetness from
    the corner of one mouth to
      another in the
        dark of night.

Our sexual mysteries.

Our alligator solitudes, our lagoon stillnesses.

Our eyes under water
   surveying the scene.

Our inability not to get up.

Our ability to stand.

The troops of horsebacked thoughts
that go galloping across and never raise
   dust or leave tracks.
Let their imprint on the ether be enough!

Our hearts as strong as the
  121 year old Frenchwoman
    from Arles who sold
  canvas to Van Gogh, and in
1995 came out with a hit CD of her
wisdom riffs.

It may look like a seahorse wrapping its

    tail around a tendril,
but its voice is Pavarotti on a
    good day, rattling the
windowpanes: *The human soul.*

Casting its
shadow on the moon.

                                                        2/22

REPLY TO A LETTER FROM A LONG-LOST FRIEND

I greet you from my deathbed.

I lie in a darkened room, listen to the
   slow ticking of day into
     night,
night into day.

Standing behind the bed, to my right, are
   multitudes of people I have
known in my life, from all different
   periods, some of them
solemn, some nonchalant, some I shared
sex or consciousness or visions of the future, or just
joked about the present, or some are my
relatives, or school acquaintances, or
people I passed on the Calle de la Reforma in
   Mexico City in 1963, walking with the
blind giant who'd fallen from a tree in his
youth and now walked with
   stick and platform shoes, because his
body was too deformed, and
almost every passerby greeted him by name, in his
long white toga and flowing black hair,
   César, blind Christ among
     exhaust fumes.

And I am tired here on my deathbed, long-lost

    brother, it is
        supported by legions of
very old angels, because as they
    transport it through the
blackened blue of eternity the bed
tilts from time to time and
      threatens to tip me off.

But perhaps it is you who've been
tipped off by now that I'm
not really on my deathbed. After so many years of
not hearing from you I thought it would be more
dramatic for you to get a letter that
    said I was. It would make my

statements more poignant to know they're my
last, last ounce of energy squeezed to
say them. But you know, in another sense, now that I

think of it a little, we do greet
each other from our deathbeds floating along on a
great Nile of consciousness, crocodile of
    forgetfulness snapping dream jaws in black
      waters all around us, our beds
floating with communicative nearness at times,
then apart, after which our
    cries to each other echo distantly

along the black river,

so I can say, yes, I

   greet you from my
deathbed in Philadelphia,

the angels carry it very slowly in the dark
and their self-illumined faces show
like full moons over the river, about a
    dozen or so of them, and they
speak to each other without sound, their
    eyelids heavy with nuance, their

white lips trembling with
   hesitant expectation.

2/26

IN THE TINIEST MIRROR

In the tiniest mirror God's smile can be seen.
In a fleck of light from a knocked off edge,
in the fragile shingle of iridescence from a
    butterfly wing, a twig of wire,
in the cutaway mid-section of a feather, a
      mustache hair, a drop of sperm, a

spot of blood, dew drop on a leaf, clover-leaf on
   Los Angeles Freeway, our twinkling
galaxy, fuzz-ball in space all twinkled with
     inner light, invisible orbits of
        planets as grindingly mindful of their
one-way tracks as a train,
details! *Details!* The

tiniest detail part of God's signature, tanta-
   lizingly spiralled, looped with
     love, strung out across a
line with gorgeous rolls and curlicues,
  an architect's angularity, a
      builder's clarity, a
        scientist's brevity,

an artist's floridity. Bravado without
    pomp, grandeur in a mouse's
      hovel of straw between walls,
in a bower-bird's turquoise knickknacks for an
   entranceway, each

detail in itself a dome of sublimity,
each leap of flea an Olympic feat,

each mirror of detail at the same time a
mirror of the whole.

                                                                              2/27

ORCHESTRATED BY ANGELS

Some people step down who sleep at
   night, others step up,
some push away in a laden barge over Lethe,
some people stand still on a lake so
polished black it reflects every
star in the sky, and farther, every planet,

some people go rigid where they are, the
   subway trains of sleep flash past them in
opposite directions on parallel track,
others peel pomegranates in the potentate's
   garden, one hand resting on a lute,

others fall asleep amid car-crash, splinters of
   lightning illuminate their
      slit-eyed faces,

others horizontal in a great waterless
   pool of lizards and sharks and
   mothers-in-law in snorkels with their
overly articulate voices even more
   distinguishable under water,
waterless water,

other people stay awake and don't think they
   ever sleep, their eyes and minds like
grindstones on which every
uncomfortable detail gets sharpened,

others wait and the smooth limousine of sleep
whooshes up and puts them in the
back seat completely upholstered in
   new-smelling black leather, fresh
     champagne at their elbows,

others lie back on a tundra so windy the
woolly coats of the Bactrian camels look like
   trees in a hurricane, great
     clumps detaching —

everyone goes into night sleep or day sleep
   differently, as in
different foreign countries with
   different cuisine and currencies,

yet a single moon-face inclines above the
slow-motion waterfall, a single
luminous sliver of smile over the most
catastrophic encounters, dreamscape or
   real girders ripping through
skin, real or unreal
   barracudas attaching nasty teeth to
     a vagabond limb,

one acknowledgement over all increases our
enlightenment even asleep,

one sound of two lips completely at peace,
flutter of eyes behind lids, flutter of
heart in the chest, finger-flutter

ever-so-slightly of hands at rest on dark covers
on the outer verge of sleep

    orchestrated by angels.

2/28

THE SKY IS RED

The sky is red.

The night is short.

My table's full of books
I haven't read.

A death's head
hovers in the air.

I've gotten up
to pee

and write
this poem.

                                         3/4

IT'S A DIFFERENT LOCATION

It's a different location from, say, a
   ten-story office building with
     evenly clipped lawn and noon sun
blindingly reflecting off the window glass
and the hurried people trying bravely to
keep to a schedule that's not theirs,

it's located always and sometimes indefinitely
elsewhere from the car kept running by the side of
the automatic teller while you
   press buttons, deposit checks, receive
     crisp twenties without seeing
       anyone,

it's even not locatable in open spaces in which
such a blue sky, inverted, would be a
pool of pellucid purity you'd expect
real dolphins to come
   splashing out of drawing
  mythological water-chariots with
    spangly nymphs singing mightily,
slow cloud-thoughts drifting across,
   sudden pinpoint lights of clarity
     making ideal outlines into
       gorgeous hologram pictures,

even in an ideal moment, in an ideal
space, with all our sensations lined up in

perfect symmetry, sights, sounds, smells
as of fresh pomegranate juice on a tropical
terrace dreaming to distant bamboo flute music,

even this is only a
genteel facade cut by the Great Diamond Cutter
Who inspires each moment and
   fashions the settings,

for actual reality takes place both deep within and
   totally elsewhere to this
cinemascope series of events,
indescribable, even though we
never tire of trying to describe it,
never tire of going toward it, desiring to
become it, shampooing it deep into our
   essence, wear it on the
 inside like a skeleton of light,
    heart atrium of deliriously high
      altitudes,

and inside the
exchange in the shopping mall,
  words over the phone at 11:30 AM,
facts and dates and the endless
addition and subtraction of numbers,
both inside these things like
  elusive seed kernels and simultaneously

outside in a wilderness of glass-like
   transparency and brilliance

the true reality within itself and generous to a fault
beckons and draws us toward it
over difficult terrain and the
bodies of those who've gone before us
sweetly resigned to being our steppingstones,

angel-faced seagulls of instantaneous
   illumination

cawing overhead.

3/4

DAWN PRAYER

I stood before my Lord at dawn
  and for a moment I was a
    fiery tropical lily, orange with
      yellow spots, a blue sky
  in front of me,
I was a pane of glass with iridescent striations,
I was a symphony orchestra under water,
I became a long shadow cast in sand of a
  city in ruins or an
    oasis withered to stalks,
I was the expression on an old woman
  watching her last grown son leave home,
for a moment I was goldfish in a
  tank aboard a yacht bound for
    China filled with
      explosives,

I stood before my Lord at dawn
on the lip-edge of creation
and I became a canyon space full of early
  fog, a panorama for clouds
    to pass in,
    shifting pastel shapes,

I prayed before God and
  became a dark river with early morning
    voices of men setting out in
      canoes — echoes, cries —

I became a space in which things happen,

I became a space where prayer happens.

3/6

CAT

The cat, so perfectly well made,
   all her tufts and natural folds just so,
     her big round perfect eyes and the
expression on her face both impassive and
     alive,

comes and interrupts my work at the table,
nibbles the end of my pen as I write,
noses me with her cool damp nose, rubs me with
her perfect fur, her perfect harmonious motions,
and she is also a universe, come from
   where she was sitting or sleeping,

she looks me in both eyes with her two round green eyes
from the center of her looking
to the center of my seeing,
stands with her two front legs stiff before her
and her body perfectly still and her
tail curled perfectly in front, and stares at me,

and she is a universe of being come
   full statured and complete to
contemplate me with whatever
consciousness she has, be it full of twitch-inducing
   bird flight memories or
slow skulking, she's down on the floor now at

three-quarter view from where I sit and she

looks up at me with the same round eyes, and
takes my looking at her as a signal and suddenly comes
back onto the table and sniffs me, then
purrs into my ear, actually
   buzzes that contented motor sound
      directly into my left aural lobe, then

goes off again, content I'm here, just as I'm
content with her smooth perambulations
   around the house, both of us

in God's full Presence.

                3/8

BLIZZARD BACCHANAL

As if the earth were to go on and on forever
    another four inch layer of snow silently covers
       time and space out the window
stretching all the way to the ocean,

icy white powder piled up on garden furniture out back
   salvaged two summers ago from
      four doors down as being
        paint-spattered but still usable,

snow covers the cars out front
lined up in all one direction, carpeted with
   white, granted an ermine blanket,
sweetly docile with iced
   windows and frozen locks, unlike
     gas-guzzling road hogs, more like
       obedient slaves,

it covers the park at the end of the street
with its wild trails over fallen tree trunks
deep in snow, growth stopped in its
   tracks under repeated onslaughts of
     angelic frosting, the
    small mammals enduring, small
       insects gathering their eggs for a
Spring resurgence or savage revenge,

the palace of pure nature wall to wall with

snow-crystals waiting for
         princely footprints, for
small quick prints of the princess to
      imprint themselves or for
long loopy chorus lines of angels to
   suddenly cavort on fresh snow in the
         little wood, pixieish

post-midnight bacchanals on
   pure white floors, under full moonlight,
time frozen still,

space as beautiful as a
   mouse ear in all this
radiance.

3/8

AT THE COMMAND OF THE SKY

At the command of the sky
   the heart beats, the hand moves
     to write, lips open
to speak or sing,

space fills to bursting with the
   helium of voice,
sudden successions of tiny gold wings
     come down,
a stairway carved of pure light
    uncollapses,

ears tune up like periscopes to hear the
   unheard, turning in
     space to the
      littlest sound,

the job there is to know
   less than you know, lest they
know you as a traitor
     and eat you,

consumed into the unseen
by unseen forces,

a sometime something passed out

   into a non-thing
until all is silent.

3/9

EMBER FALLING THROUGH SPACE

If we are an ember falling through space
with the chance
   we'll ignite and be a
bright spark against blackness
    endlessly falling, and for a
moment endlessly bright, incandescent
melodious ember, dead thing reanimated
like a premature season, confla-
   gration in slow motion,

contentment of being as a docile thing
transformed into flocks of tropical birds
with blinding bright plumage,
one thought turning in space
expanded to space itself, all-encompassing, one
   heartbeat
  become at a stroke
the flutter of everything's pulse on earth
    unfolding like water spray
as it falls from a height down to rocks
  across death's own distance,

vibrating harp strings
stretched across an abyss
vibrantly singing,

if we are this ember and if we are
  slowly falling, now like a

piano with fiery keys, tiny pyramids of
    ice on each one, now like
spears of ice diagonally heading toward
fiery hearts, now like
the growth of spears of grass in a solid wall of
    earthly nourishment,

an ember which falls in only
    half-life ignition, then
suddenly fully ignites, reflecting in its light

laborious Mongol migrations across
    stepping places on rapidly
        eroding isthmuses,
fame and humiliation rapidly alternating in
    the life of one man, held up as
a King on Monday, laid in a box on Friday
    cold as a stone,

yet for this indefatigable moment
like a window in Paradise that looks out on
God's tree again from a respectful
    distance,
God's knowledge
like a fountain of bronze rainbows so liquid
fish of all stripes can swim in it
    arching their backs like Japanese bridges,

it continues across in the air,
its light containing the
    orbits of both

   darkness and silence,
its transitory flight containing both
action and stillness,

it descends so
slowly it might be rising,
a house in a hurricane might fall as
slowly through space as this
ember we are,
but with its
   windows dark,

this is a flashing window in space that looks
   both ways before
     falling, heavenward constantly
and earthward through
   fear of falling,

if we are an ember like an empire of
spines of radiant glorification and
precise definition of joy
   uncontainable and so
     inflammable, a tiny
inconsequential splinter of light become the
sun,

then we are as we are
falling through the air

held in suspended animation
in the middle of nowhere.

                                                       3/12

MIND PIANO

> *Who you are is dust*
> *& what you are is immortal*
>   — Michael Hannon

The mind piano of autobiographical detail
plays in a back alley, picks out
   lame requests and favorite show tunes,
occasionally attempts Rachmaninoff,
makes a healthy run at Bach,

yet something about autobiography always seems
forced, describing not somebody else, so
   much as nobody ever, or else
it's a description from the inside
   projecting outward that
ends up by putting new fictional flesh on
   autobiographical bones, so the

person who's the subject now
looks better, talks better, is
   much much sexier or
     devout,

but a Papier-mâché, gryphon's head
could have been lowered over the
subject's own serviceable cranium,
it wouldn't make much difference.

Since the perishable self is

essentially transparent enough for
flocks of starlings to fan through going
   north or south, or the
spray from Victoria Falls to catapult
   rainbows through doing
      death defying acrobatics,

the self is a kind of moisture in the
   air ultimately, a kind of
smell of baking in a tumble-down
   rural village in the Balkans, a kind of
distant music out a parked car window
   in bright green country, or even
a mistaken identity in a center city
police raid behind a paint-peeling door,

the self is as elusive as a
Middle Eastern smuggler in a fake
  blond beard on a subway
    with a package under his arm,

and yet all these subterfuge selves —
birds, waterfall, humidity, sinister criminal —
are all turquoise glow on the back of a
ruby tree by the milky river of Paradise,
golden powder filtering through the
  air near the swan pavilion,
a gorgeous note, higher than usual,
held by a black soprano in the
   air over a silver lake
     in the Alps,

the single self is multiple and picturesque,
atmospheric and as minutely particular as
the spots on a moth's wing
or the freckles on a cricket
   happily mating under the
      leaf of a periwinkle,

and autobiography of this elusive cosmic entity
both misses its vastness and
overstates its accomplishments, which are
nothing at all, vapor in the air,
for true autobiography is the unvarnished
History of God out of all time and space,
non-chronological, expanded to every
   known horizon,
    a web-like tent of all human
      exhalations drawn down over
nomadic encampments of shadow,
or the echo of a sound still reverberating
   along mountainous
     goat-filled crags
long after the land mass that initially made them
has settled down and is now full of
   fir trees and wildlife
      basking in the summer sun.

A light in the sky.

A scent in the air of a certain night.

A shadow on rippling water

    you can see
        down into the depths of,

and the depths are there,
wearing our faces and
trembling with our heartbeats,

and a lone black horse comes
    out of them, shakes the

water from its mane and

stands suspended for a full minute

before charging down the hill.

                                        3/21

GOD'S IN THE DETAILS

In Spokane, Washington, at the corner of
   Lily and Tenth, on a dark night,
rain puddles reflecting Victorian casements and
    cornices, a flutter in the air, flashing
star-shaped yellow burst, Amelia closes her eyes and it's
still there, writing subtle words
   inside her eyelids: *"Valse suave,*
      Monette, valse vite!"
She holds onto a railing and feels like flying.

At the back of a warehouse in Copenhagen,
behind a latticework shadows of blond wooden
platforms stored on end, Elgar feels inside his
soft cotton undershirt, brushes his
   hands across his nipples, leans back and
inhales the entire afternoon, gnats and
    ants included, shifts his weight,
becomes the sky, hears the words, in Danish:
"It is finished, it is hollow, it is full, it is
endless."

In the Amazon, deep in the forest known by the
   locals as "Locus of Green Spirits,"
a grandfather blows through a blowgun up into a
    tree to the amazement of his
      grandson, and a poisoned arrow
pierces the skin of a howling monkey who
immediately leads the chase for three miles

across the treetops until, exhausted, he
falls dead at their feet. *"Machoaca labita cala"* the
   grandfather says, and they hoist it
     onto a branch and start the
long trek home. Everything routine, except
the boy catches a glimpse of the god. Between
   two trees. In shadow. The long
     face. The distant laughter.
The wild, red eyes. The green hair.

Between trains in downtown Beirut, watching
   herself in a department store window
reflected between mannequins dressed in newest
     Paris fashions, Amira
suddenly sees herself multiply like stop photographs of
opening moth-wings, accordian-like, of
   herself in various blurred
     replicas, her face on each a
full moon smiling like a radiant queen, and the
sound of the world drained away for a
moment replaced by celestial sighing,
   cosmic intake of breath,
and she had to steady herself on a
     lamppost until it passed.

And it did pass, as all these
brief epiphanies passed through their
subjects, or more precisely, their objects,
leaving them briefly
as wide open as morning mountains under
   brash sunlight,

these momentary revelations entirely
   vaporizing them and turning them
not quite inside-out nor upside-down, but

song came more readily to their lips afterward,

a fountain dripped in shadow from
   somewhere deep within each one of them
that refreshes anyone who hears of them or
hears in detail, in divine detail, what

befell them, whatever it was that
   filled them beyond their
     usual capacity, and then

        passed on.

                                        3/29

WATCHING PEOPLE PASS BY

You wouldn't think, looking at people with their
insignificant sizes and seemingly improvised
    shapes, that they contain
mile high shale cliffs, clefts in rocks that drop
  deep down into canyons, glassy
      divides fully populated by
choirs, flora and fauna of the most
diverse and sophisticated kind, as well as
all the anomalies, tiny insects with
    human faces and the antlers of moose,
trees taller than the tallest sequoias whose
bark hangs long like the hair of great-grandfathers
or Spanish moss,

that these bustling folk speeding past
intersections on poorly shod feet with
umbrellas and perambulators
should contain multitudes, not only of
   peoples but also of
     weathers, sleet and snow, icy rain as well as
tropical humidity no amount of fanning with
elephant-ear leaves of the glossiest green could
assuage, and showers of insects, lagoons of
   pure silver in grottos of blue and gold,
winds that sound like the dawn of the airplane
attempting to take off only to
     land in a heap of
       struts and broken body-parts,

weathers, landscapes, worlds imagined and
   unimaginable, each with its
     guardian and its sage
sitting alone in an inner sanctum
   awaiting our return,

we see these people run by on their way to miss their
train or disgruntle their employer
and we'd never know they're at the
crossroads of territories more exotic than
 India under the Mogul Empire, or
China when the emperor was at the
center of the Forbidden City
   unviewable by common eyes, gazed on only by
opium mothers, consumptive princesses and
eunuchs, that inside these

stressed individuals are decisions each moment more
momentous than the last, to elect the
Hawk Representative to the tribal council,
marry their daughters to the wealthiest man in
   Pompeii, or
move heaven and earth to find the inner
   certitude that brings the
     peace that passeth understanding

as one foot leaves the curb, the other
clicking smartly behind, arms
swinging nonchalantly, head tilted,
   eyes averted,
     mind wandering,

heart beating, the constantly remembering heart

beating out the divine syllables in code both
    secret and well-known that create by
the propulsion of their sound
the smallest atom awaiting the command to
    become a rose,
the greatest mountain awaiting the command to
bow its head under God's power, fleecy
    clouds passing by,

sky an endlessly shifting panorama
inside the separate outlines

of these hurrying people passing by.

4/1

ANGELS SING

If something could assuage the strange
   pain we all feel in a part of us,
the gnawing feeling that we
   don't do enough or aren't enough
before some giant monolith of consciousness
that perpetually judges us and finds us
   wanting, wanting

that funny jigsaw piece to either materialize completely or
get completely lost, the gnawing

sensation that accompanies most of our
breathing, is perhaps part of our
biological condition, sensation that originates in the
center of our physical being, fingers ending
   inconclusively at their tips, arms and legs
dangling inconclusively at the
     hinges of their acrobatic dangle,
thoughts pinched in a bottle or tunnel of
   unrelenting constraint, perhaps only
     molecular, physical, part of having a

physique at all, that needs
   preening and pruning, the upkeep is
     overwhelming at times (haircuts, lose weight,
keep from wheezing), when we are

growing entities, like cactus on a

windowsill in a ceramic pot in
　　full sunlight, almost
　　　　unnoticed until you see some
protuberance sticking straight up
boding new growth of more
cactus-like entities, we are

not static with fixed eyes staring
straight ahead like the folk from Sumer,
aswim in cosmos and filled with
　　cosmos, we
miscalculate depths and underestimate
　heights, pushing off anyway,

eyes always focusing on some
point of light ahead of us,

if something could assuage
the strange pain of all this,
would it mean the ascent be not
attained, that we wouldn't hear

　　　angels sing?

4/3

JOURNEY

You cross the girdered bridge where
   two tall cypresses stand, walk slowly over
black water rolling under you,
go past the lengthy wall made of stone blocks and
   carved human heads, walk down the hill until the
      wall gets taller, the
city gate now stands before you,
twin stone lions at either side with their
live topaz eyes almost electric in their
   beams, you
go in nonchalantly as if you've
   gone through this gate before, the
city opens up here, you're conscious of

sunny blue sky for the first time, scattershot of
     tiny birds like shooting
  vocal flowers through the air, making a kind of
scent with their innocent motions,

the streets are lined with shops selling
baskets in the shapes of wild animals, pottery in the
   shapes of grotesque men and women, food and
      spices brought from the literal
ends of the earth. Everyone who sells things here
wears coarse blue hooded robes and
hides his or her face, no one speaks, you might as
   well be floating, the street ends,
checkerboard pavement begins, and in the

distance a forest, thick, black-shadow-splotched,
filled with forest-sounds, tweets and
   creakings, you walk on through stands of
robust pine and fir trees,
come to a clearing, O

   come to this clearing
you ancient ones, you newborn ones,
and on a small wooden altar see a
disk that is
sometimes a mirror, sometimes a
   telescope lens, sometimes a
window looking out into the trees, green
  open space all
   around it, you
contemplate the scene and gaze through the
round disk and see
your journey reversed, back through the
forest the way you came, back through the
fascinating trinket-stalls, the gate whose
lions now come alive and
   lope away, thin haunches
working like rope against a wharf,

back across black water to the
beginning of this poem and back from the
page to the reader and to the

writer who at this single moment
are one and the same.

                                                    4/5

THE WORLD

There's a big ship cutting through the water
   to Singapore —
I'm not on it.

There's an example of domed fantasy architecture
   that looks like the building is hovering in
     space —
I'm not in it.

There's a tunnel that cuts beyond the
   images of this world into the endlessly
     swirling image-sources of the next —
I'm not through it.

There's a tropical paradise of giant flowers in the
   shapes of velvety jugs of delirious nectar
    and beaches so white they're blue —
I'm not from it.

There's a world of rapine and mistrust, of
   the fiery licking tongues of war and
    retribution, of cautious reconciliation and
     occasional majesty and beauty —
I'm not of it.

                                           4/10-11

NUDE, I BEAR YOU

Nude, I bear you across the land
with the white cloth under you in my arms
fluttering as we rush through the air
across cities into wastelands and
    empty lots, across bridges strung with
lights, across America and all the other
       continents, your

arms around my neck, your
white legs dangling,

we disappear down winding alleyways, into
labyrinth parts of towns meandering up hills
and stand briefly on peaks under
pale moonlight,

we go down into the noise of the cities the way
great ships sink into their own froth
and I bear you past people not noticing and
occasional children who point us out and
   cry, cry out, yell out the names of their
own popular heros, and we pass,

we disappear into the mouths of forests
in search of the wise grandmother
who remains invisible while she
    instructs us on the usages of leaves,

we pass fishermen and their children helping
   with nets at blue twilight,

we pass great economic institutions and
   momentous political agreements
and the white cloth both covers and reveals you

in your flush of life, in your
shapely limbs and face of beauty, face of
life, eyes of solar life, with your

white lips that have
touched moonlight.

4/11

HANDS TO THE SIDES OF OUR HEADS

"Because I have senses
Fake and primitive
And cannot grasp what really Exists —"
— Gunnar Ekelof

1

I have the feeling, the pervasive and
   nagging premonition or sensation
that if I were to take realty as real,
suddenly have the epiphany that
   this is God-drenched reality full of light and
in itself, with all its surface contours, circles, squares,
      right angles and oblique
         encounters, a spray of
light equally pouring up through both of us,
and I could see through it as one might see past a
doorway with a beaded curtain, each bead a
   jeweled prism that

      accentuates the Seen and heightens its
reality, gives each thing a halo of rainbows or
dimensional resonance at least, makes of things
   objects at the same time more
      substantial and more transparent,
next world and this world joined in a single vision,
walnut shell cracked to catch light, closed to
   ensure its perfect preservation,
roads that almost moan to us their

    actual destinations, doors that almost
open of their own accord to let us enter into
peaceable territories.

To sit down comfortably as if admitting any reality at
    all to this world were not a betrayal,
its winds and lesser breezes, its
    meetings and departures, its chance
        operations and long-time decreed
            inevitable conclusions.

If I could
stand in the icy glare of this place and not feel
my major part not buying it for a second as
anything more than a pictorial passageway into
pictures more radiant and
alive than these will ever be —

    this is a passing mood —

to see a wall as truly a wall, a
    floor and ceiling as
completely and eternally themselves without
a barrage of insubstantial white
    horses furiously galloping though it all
to reach the sea, snort and
    thrash in its waves, flicking their
graceful white tails, shaking waterbeads out of
    their manes, fiery black and
blue and green eyes like
    sea-beacons independently

    crossing beams.

2

As if, just behind things,
leaning a bright forehead against their
  inner wall, the angel of the
      Absolutely Real
availed itself in space, and with a
   cool lunar smile on its face, its
sweet cat-like face, held the
immediate sensation of reality
  in abeyance on its lips,

expelling it into the air from time to
   time to heighten our awareness of reality's
crystalline shapes.

Am I a disappointed child?
(At 56 I still feel uncomfortable
   around grownups) —
Is it more fervent fantasy I desire?
Instead of street-lamps, golden orbs?
Instead of traffic lights, green and red
   demons exchanging places?
Are there too few fountains, I mean giant
   fountains with craggy rocks or heroic
     statuary spouting up grand
fans of water a dazzling sunlight can
      filter through? Too few on our

streets, too few in our
neighborhoods, too few wagons going by filled with
singing children, too few
wild animals prowling peacefully through our
   world, panthers at our feet while we
read or write, occasionally
     gazing up at us with
         yellow eyes.

As if a figure stood in shadow behind the utmost
reality of things and could
   will their greater intensity to
      convince us. But this world

always dangles

just out of reach.

3

It all collapses neatly into a house of cards,
accordions into interlocked cascades,
reality dazzles the eye and heart like
   rays from an exploding star, sound waves from a
tidal tsunami rolling in from heaven,
it all ripples, wavers, snaps in the wind,
rises up in splendiferous breakers, hangs in
frozen beads down the winter window, breaks
   open like a lake opening its one eye under the
gaze of the sun, like a mirror blinking open

under the unblinking gaze of God.

We move in it and it moves as we move,

   windows become filled with heart-stoppingly
   gorgeous sights, castles made out of
   molecules as fantastic as the one by mad King Ludwig
   on those pinnacle Austrian peaks, but these molecules
   form mosquitos landing on our arms,
   green dragonflies hovering over a lotus pad,
   light-motes filtering down through the afternoon,
   the aroused sex of a small mouse inside an
      earth-hole approaching its missus,
   the twirling petal of a rose before twisting off,
   the pale face of John Keats who
      leans toward me now in his
        front parlor to hand me his
   latest ode and asks me
     what I think, and I say: "The pink
   of sunlight and the blue of the morning sky
   have never been better captured,"
   and he smiles and winks his eye,

   and reality shivers with ague, blusters with
      a tubercular cough, flutters a
        laudanum eyelid like that of
          Coleridge, goes down a
   long dark passageway hoping to come out
   years later fully recovered,

   the majestic interlocking of star shapes and

happy crescents is the warp and weave of the
Pattern-Maker's pattern, and the

sighing and disbelief at how overwhelming it
   so often is are the

song of praise we send back to the Origin
and our gratitude to the One God Who
supervises the
falling of each leaf and the rippling of their
   delicate edges, the
painting of each frost branch
   and the prismatic glitter of their sheen,

the rich billion-part harmony of voices and
   shapes in a symphony so colossal
 we hear only a corner of its echo and feel
far from its reality, until our own

heartbeats join in
with one word or many,
one song or fragment of song,
one note or silent whisper,

one vision of the whole not obstructing the vision of its
Creator

raising our hands to the sides of our heads
in awe.

4/15-19

NATURE POETRY

Nature poetry is still just nature imagined.
The texture of a leaf, sun in a green glade,
   smell of birch bark, sound of twig-snap underfoot
are all language constructs,
words with green sprout-snouts peeping out
     from around them.

The men down there in the
   bright orange rubber boat going down
silver frothing rapids
are just words, loudly reverberating along
     early morning canyon walls.

The man falling over in his rubber suit,
sinking in boiling foam, dragged
   suddenly ecstatically deep down
in black and white water,
gliding through his life, swooshing along
   his own private gallery, saying
goodbye to the pictures, hands by his
sides like an arctic seal,
dreaming of gliding in a sky rather than a
deep pit of water, eyes blinded by the
     fury of quicksilver,

is only a mortality of words, not a
real life lost of a man whose
house will be empty of him on Monday, whose

wife and children will grieve, put a
   rock pile by the side of the
cataract where he fell,

and yet he's also all who've fallen, all who've
   desired release, who've braved the
ragged edge electrified with God's own lightning,

all who've blindly gone into the deeps to see for himself
and have ended up as he has
slapped on the smooth bottom of a rock basin,
propelled up along a glassy side,
tossed back into the sunlight on the surface,
barely alive, bobbing in his
   yellow rubber suit,

verb of forgiveness,
noun of celestial endlessness,
comma or exclamation point —

Look! There in the sunlight!

4/26

MAYBE NOBODY'S REALLY HAPPY

Maybe nobody's really happy.

Maybe the King of Siam, seated on his ornate throne,
wishes he were a kid again
   hiding in his mother's brocades.

Maybe everyone fears God's judgement, retribution like
   hot ingots falling from an
     open closet door,
ravenous eagles clawing their real way into our
   bowels from a simple nightmare,
the unsettled feeling of accomplishments unaccomplished,
words misplaced, thoughts astray, feelings
   overabundant or inappropriate.
The canopy of sky pulled down.
The earth with its aromatic verdure
   rejecting us.
Even the saint in his sunlit room at
   midnight wanting to be
    more in the next world than
in this one, where the grass is
definitely and eternally greener.

Perhaps everyone wants to be in a warm bath of
   infinite sorrow, then
kick a hole in its bottom and be
floating in a sky full of stars.

Maybe no one is really that happy for very long,
although at about six o'clock this afternoon,
   a late May afternoon sunlight very
      golden and glistening but
         muted in the room, as if in a
deep forest, the carpets and furniture alike
glowing in it, and after a day like a
   real spring day after a long, hard winter,
air warm, doors open, having done most of the
  things I wanted to do, fix the front
water-pipe that broke off in the blizzard from
frozen water inside, and I planted the
seven tomato plants given to me on Friday —

for a few moments I suddenly did feel
happy, buoyant, not depressed about my
   job or financial worries, or
dying before I complete the
Great Work, whatever that is,
   before reaching Allah, before
becoming in this world a pool of
   genial quicksilver to reflect the
most light possible, turn my old familiar
     shopworn selves
inside-out indelibly and forever, to be

generous and benign, grandfatherly-grandmotherly,
  open-hearted to all, thinking of
everyone before myself, illumined —

yet maybe no one is happy for long,

everyone wants to cry his or her eyes out,
shout into the nightmare, hold the edges as
   hard as possible before they
      crumble away, and we,
blown husks, crumble with them —

maybe everyone feels indefinite, ill-defined,
   ambiguous, manic-depressive,

the great elk blanket of blue snow
covering our hearts like a season of privation

when it seems
even a tiny drop of true happiness in our cup

would quench our thirst forever.

5/5

WHEN SOMEONE

When someone hasn't the usual impediments to
   human existence: self-doubt, hesitance to
     act directly, lack of a
radiant inner compass, irrational
   fearfulness, inner agony about
innumerable things, actual
     physical pain, a warped ego,

and walks forward with faithful confidence,
moves with harmonic human grace,

we are exhilirated.

                                                   5/8

CONTEMPLATION ON THE ROCKS

1

I think I'll stay up here among the rocks —
   ah, these beautiful rocks,
  each with the face of an angel!
I've had enough of earthly life.
I've run down too many of other people's corridors,
    I've burst into too many of
      other people's rooms.
Now I want to wear only
  clouds and rainbows.
No one else needs to appear in my mirror.

The deer run to greet me.
The water in the stream runs down the hill,
   laughing.
The blue of the sky opens its eyes as wide as it can
to look deep into my heart.
So I don't hold back anything, since no
   corner remains hidden.
I'll wait here for low-flying vultures
  to cast me their cold glances.

Alone on a stone outcrop, day or night,
I'll read crevices and stars
chapter by chapter, deconstruct each
   grassblade
     twitch by twitch.

The ease with which people help themselves to death
is frightening. So much darkness
   gone to waste, when it could
backdrop something truly bright and make it
     radiant!

I'll collect breezes.
I'll know which way the wind blows.
I'll sing the song of the
   devoured rose.

I know how it goes.

2

No more number, no more
   ones and twos, no plus a hundred or
   minus a hundred, no more
divided by's or multiplied by's. I'll let
God's breaths be my chronometer.

The trees inch up around us undetected.
The earth shambles this way and that
   beneath us.
Now we're on top, now underneath.
I salute the starry roof of this
   underground cavern.

When light comes we dance.
When light goes we lie down.

Primitive man still finds comfortable positions
   within us. Heart a
reflecting device. God's Face

what appears there.
The small birds darting from tree to tree.
   They know the routes to
     fulfillment. Only
take what they need.

If we let our eyes roam
they'll decipher the indecipherable tablets
   God's placed all around us.
The language of doves. The
esoteric language of earth worms.
It all slows down to a sonorous drone.

God's breaths our chronometer.

3

The rarified air up here is good to the ears.
You hear only the clicks of leaves as they
   snap from boughs and
     ping like bells when they
   land on earth to die,
every creak of pebble or rock as it
   settles in next to a neighbor,
   shale sliding, a creature
disturbing the dust, pushing aside a

  miniscule clod.

The air up here is a vehicle for the direct arc from
meaning to apprehension,
the sky is the silence after an
  orchestra's crescendo, the white on the
   screen after the picture's gone.

Everything has room in it.
In it, everything sings.
Every word in the heart
is as clear an enunciation of
  itself as the
 feeling along foot by foot of a
  caterpillar on a branch, or the
deep roar of a midnight beast
  hungry at the moon.

The sky covers all with utmost serenity
and listens.

Not an inert bystander,
but the mother of us all.

No cloud passing in it
 unloved.

Assuaged
by a loving hand.

            5/11-12

FIRST-HAND SUNLIGHT, FIRST-HAND ROCK

In any moment, like a blue glass swan
   perched on a tall thin rod,
we should, hearts open, be able to see
God's Light streaming in the windows of our
   eyes and splashing its love-carpets on the
cool chambers of our heartbeats.

I'm sitting at the dining room table, late at night,
house asleep, black cat creaking on a
   paper bag full of newspapers on a chair
behind me, refrigerator maintaining harmonic
drone to the atmosphere, and I'm

thinking of old poems, old unfoldings of
   gorgeous landscapes populated by
purple mountains, majestic silver lakes,
clouds in profile moving across the blue
sea of the sky,

landscapes unapproachable by any vehicle but
imagination, landscapes in golden
   flames, landscapes of roads through
dark forests encased in sudden domes of
green ice, landscapes the size of a
   thimble overturned to display the
intricate weaving of fiber and web, moonlight and
   mud underneath, as slow as a
piano solo with big chords,

igniting something half-remembered in the heart
but anxiously longed for over countless years
and perhaps even centuries, a longing that
    threads through generations,
a flooding with planetary darkness, a
floating out across somber marshes,
a joining of earth and horizon in a
transubstantiating flash that makes of us

indelibly spiritual doers or non-doers of actions
in which we, as hollow landscapes, let the
Majestic Doer perform and
    complete us
with no effort from Him, our own eyes full of

first-hand sunlight reflecting off
    first-hand rock.

                                              5/15

WE HAVE COME A LONG WAY

We have come a long way on a difficult journey,
  marking our path with a
    Taj Mahal here, an atrocity there,
a crystal palace on a green hill with
  shimmering peacock windows,
a war of bright red dust that enters hearts and
    turns them to brick,
a glamorous celebration, a ditch filled with
  skeletons.

A lamp sits on a windowsill in Brazil,
a painter closes his eyes to sleep.
Music down in the dungeons of the soul
    sounds like salvation.
A voice so thin gnats catch in it,
not a child's, not quite an adult's,
someone dying, making a speech to the ceiling,
saying farewell to the insulating tiles,
a voice of someone coming into an empty house,
then suddenly realizing,
a voice that's been locked out of the cheeriness
  of human commerce,
sails a hat on a lucid stream
until birds pick it up
and place it on the head of the priest of a
  pagan cult
decorated with toucan feathers.

We are haunted by spiders that have
    never woven a web,
by a building that never casts a shadow,
by a hole that has no depth, a
    sky that doesn't ascend,
air that space occupies, solid as rock,

we are haunted by people we've known and loved
who don't recognize us on the street,
haunted by mirrors that show a
    tall cypress tree against a black hillside.

We've come a long way on a difficult journey,
turned sharp corners around the
    Renaissance with its giant frescoes,
        its stone palaces,
made a detour around trench warfare, mustard gas,
    Hiroshima, Touret's Syndrome,
fallen in love with images gone in a flash,
filled arenas with adulators and flatterers
      for führers and rock stars,
haunted later by a smile that stays in the air,
by the sound of helicopter blades over a
    tropical delta,
of a subway car caroming around a
      dark curve underground,

haunted by a clogged tear duct, by a
word that refuses to come out, by a
heart that beats but will not break.

                                                  5/17-18

A VERSION OF PETRARCH

A white doe on green
grass appeared to me with two gold horns
between two rivers in a laurel's shade,
the sun rising in embryonic season.

Her look was so superbly sweet
that I dropped everything to follow her,
like a miser whose trouble seeking treasure
is made easier by deep delight.

The words "Don't Touch Me" around her beauteous neck
were written in diamond and topaz.
"My Caesar was pleased to set me free."

The sun was already halfway through its turn,
my eyes were strained by looking, but not done,
when I fell into the water and she was gone.
                 — Petrarch (Rime Sparse 190)

TREES, FOR ALL THEIR BEAUTY

Trees, for all their beauty, even
   the sounds they make rustling in breezes,
don't recite what's actually going on in their
   souls, the pictures with music in words
that poignantly or powerfully
express their momentary condition
   ticking in the river of eternity,

nor do the objects around us, tables and
chairs, they're not inclined to
   let us know what's
     passing in their souls about
standing in a certain spot in the room
as daylight passes into golden afternoon
or who sat in them, or nearly sat,

the walls of our houses are mute, the
   doors let us pass through in silence,
their air is ubiquitously patient and
   usually well-mannered to the point of
absolute quiet,

therefore poets like to read or recite out
   loud either to themselves or with the
loving participation of other ears,
they love the scintillations in space and
   the quadraphonic resonances that seem as if
called into play from farther

    out in space of forces and entities always
there in latent possibility but not
animated concretely until a poem catches them.

Poets love the window that opens as if
   sunning the curtains in the
     heart and letting their tresses
buoyantly billow outside the window's confines
when words from the human soul are
articulated into feeling states and
  musical thinking states,

poets love the camaraderie of other souls
listening, letting aromas rise from the
deep well of words that make of both
reader and listener a
  neutral sensitivity to the
    event of the poem, its own
sizzle and electric current
lighting up its self-contained, returnable
and inexhaustibly renewable world,

repeated vocally, catching in the net of sound
cast now, at the present moment,
the partial original voice of the poet who
  wrote the poem, plus
the sonic echoes of humankind's voices of
   enlightened humanity all around us
     timelessly, or sad humankind, or
furious and impatient humankind, or
humankind so drunk with realization of the Divine

in direct encounter
that someone's heart has opened its mouth in
    the depths and out has poured

these very words, no others, these very
sounds of words and shapes of words and
colors of words in nature and brought with
our most human voice now into this room, a

lovely resonance that links us, eagerly
wrapping its arms around our hearts

to let us enjoy the glow that rises there.

                                                                          5/21

A NEW STONE

A house with a heart shaped like a gas
burns down.
Now all that's left is a
   woman in gray cloak who walks
back and forth in the wreck.

A lead pipe lies twisted on the ground.
The snake family ponders its dead.
Dust filters down.

Here is burnt sunlight, crisp and brown.
A letter burst into flame:
*"Up until now I've been well. By the
time you read this I'll be in
Hong Kong. Our time was
great. I walk in the dawn."*

The frame of the house will grin.
A drawer in a back room unsticks and
    falls open.
A white bird flutters free. Has flown.

You don't know what good news
   disaster may bring.

On a platter sits a new stone.

5/22

WRONG SIDE OF THE BED

I've gotten up on the wrong side of the bed
and found myself sitting on a
    peaked roof floating downstream in a
      flood, a jar of
gherkins in my hand, playing softball with a
   gray goose, optimistic of the
      outcome. We're
both outlined in a fine fuzz of icicles,
the cold air hitting our bodies like a
   buzz saw. But we're
smiling. The
   flood waters are bright red, bright
     Biblical red. I don't dare
put my finger in to see what the
   red comes from, and the
goose is showing signs of restlessness,
    which means I could be
      left alone, scanning the
sky for a speck of friendship.

I suddenly wonder where I am, more than
where I'm going. Where I'm
going is coming over me so fast,
like a large tunnel of corrugated steel,
or even like a thin rubber film that
   pulls over me from the bottom
     up, glistening whitishly in the
dwindling light. A

deer floats past, keeping its head out of
    water, working its legs,
eyeing me with beautiful black eyes full of
fear and comradeship.
"We've come from the same place," they say to me,
"and where we're going
is where the memory of all this
    sculpts character to
        perfection." I
certainly hope so, I think to myself, as my
head returns to the black
   pillow, as dawn birds,
like the sound of beaded curtains shaken,
chirp and sing outside in
    extended space
       in all directions

in the swimming interconsistency
   of time.

                                               5/23

DAWN SONG

It is dawn, and the bird outside
   has beat me to praising.
With such a fine voice as his, lariats of
    watery chortle, with the
deepest possible innocence of nature, its
    musical implacability, his
song must be
playing glass xylophones along the
   margins of heaven, while mine,

hastily stuffed into any old envelope, has to
arrive there by the greatest of angelic
   postal routes, probably with
postage due.

As part of the earth is falling away
   by rotational gravity, sliding
back into shadow, as the
sunlight lights up the world with
    pinpricks of incandescence,
a blanket of bird-like praise must be
almost visibly lifting
like an awed facial expression
   off the newly shining surface of the globe.

Each heart's like that.

Each heart must be able to see the

    lake of mercury spreading out between the
        two mountains
in the earliest light of dawn, and the
    Divine Face of Magnitude
        reflected in that lake,
and the heart's song of praise at that sight
must take flight almost unawares,
    each mote of expression
        falling upward with the same
elation that gravity uses to pull things
    down.

The bird outside has been joined by a
chirping chorus less melodic but more
intricately orchestrated, while I've been
sitting on the edge of my bed at 5 A.M.
trying to bounce words off clouds.

Birds just hop and sing.

Only God actually does anything.

                                                5/24

ANSWERED PRAYER

I think God's answered one of my most
   fervent prayers: Time has been made
to go slower. I don't know

if it's for everyone or just for me, and I don't
know yet (I'll have to institute some precise scientific
   observations) if it's really happening
(although my watch and all the surrounding
clocks that become visible to us throughout the
   day can't be lying) or only
seeming to happen.

I noticed it this morning. Got up at
   8:30, slowly, read over my last poem,
the one written after the dawn prayer this morning,
turned and dozed a little, a few
   minutes maybe, got up, remembered I
needed to type out some reactions to
a manuscript someone gave me, did so, went out into my
little back garden, watered the tomato
   plants, looked back at my window and saw the
three sunflower seedlings pressing their leafy faces against
the inside of the glass where I'd
put them in their pots until they were
   big enough to be planted outside and survive
ravenous squirrels, they seemed to be
   beseeching me to plant them so they could
thrive in the sun, so in my pajamas still, I

got a trowel and planted the three sunflowers
   next to the split bamboo fence, patting the
dirt around them gently, staking their
   limp stems to thin green stakes,
watered them as well, looked at my watch,

it was only 9:15!

It had seemed like forever!

Usually we start doing things, a little time
   passes, and it's about two or
      three hours later!

I noticed it again tonight, that for once time is
slowing down to a manageable pace, or rather
doing something at a manageable pace doesn't
   take as long, where you think your
life is passing so fast it almost has that
visual flutter of faces in the window of a
   moving train.

Could it be true? Is it age that's
   putting its sweet hobnailed boot
      on my head? Forcing me into a
more gradual, savoring mode?

How great it would be not to be rushed all the
time, to become a Saint Francis hoeing his
   garden: When someone asked him

what he'd do if he were told he had only
one more hour to live, he answered:

"Keep hoeing."

5/25

FIRST ONE ANGEL

First one angel, then another, until
   the whole sky's full.
There's a notion!

Outside the door now, drops.
While I've been asleep the whole world's been
   workin'.
Railroad tracks shoot off into the distance.
   Buds. Trees.
Towers teeter on the earth's round surface.
   Horses fly in a breeze.

Miracles each moment unfreeze.
Imagine the juxtaposition:
Jackals on heads of state. Let the
   light shine
     on em'!

Liars wear heads of snakes.
Roses in full bloom
   become children's faces.
Fresh and aromatic. Lit by
   the moon.

I think a star fell in my
   mouth while I was asleep!

Which country's been turned

   into a herd of sheep?
What prairies caught fire?

What postcards
   flutter in the breeze?

What father sees his son for the first time
and doesn't weep?
His daughter for the first time,
and doesn't look
   into his heart, so deep?

This body cuts me off from the crowd.
It's the vehicle and the obstacle
and my shroud.

But a heartbeat by itself, in space, all
   alone, faceless and bodiless,
     regular, never asleep!

That would be a golden voice
   over the deep.

5/27

BABY DAWN BLUE

I'll take the baby dawn blue of the
   sky for my mental terrain
and early morning songbirds for my heartbeat,
first faint sunrays for the gleam in my eye
and the way the wind blows as my gait.

Walking through the world as bodiless as cloud,
but like light on a meadow at noon
   the impact I make on my surroundings,
let me take this cosmos in my stride, Lord,
an ocean in each pocket, my legs straddling
   continents as easily as a fence.

Wring out the violence, digest its toxic elements
   in an immune system strong as an ox.
Life is cool petals on our eyes and song on the tongue
and sweet knowledge at our fingertips
as transparent and necessary as air.

                                                                    5/30

THE ALCHEMIST'S LAPSE

for Michael Green

Peacocks strut in the courtyard
  shouting their obscenities, their cries of despair,
rather like humans. The withered
alchemist yawns, stretching thin arms in
ample sleeves, eyeglasses falling from his
nose into the mixture,
his face freezes in terror, but down they
   go, liquifying, rims and all.

Steam starts developing, the left ear-piece
    disappears, fog ensues, the chamber
fills with a greenish smoke: *Poof!*

Or actually, ten minutes of intense
   bubbling, a kind of slow-motion "poof,"
and the smoke clears as if a blade had
wiped it away, the alchemist
slowly coming around, holding his nose
at the sulphurous stench
*(although he had to admit it was also of
hyacinths and burnt cinnamon toast, and
at dead center of the smell an
undefined, undefinable scent that recalled
a childhood boating expedition where he remembers
trailing his hands in petal-strewn water at dusk),*

and he looks into the absolute clarity
and sees gold!

He'd done all the tediously exacting
   work day in and day out for
thirteen years until now, he'd lost
friends and wealth and health, as they say,
in its dogged pursuit, Winter after Winter
opened their cold fists into Springs and
spread their palms flat into balmy Summers
but the transformation of crass matter into
   gold had eluded him. But when the

glasses fell from his face
and be became lost, plunged into a dazzle of
   fuzziness, then!
      Pure gold.

Inside the green smoke a hundred habitations had
risen and gone under, a hundred
times of peace had given way to war, a
   hundred tall mountains
eroded into hills and bloomed
   up again into mountains, mountains so
ancient and comfortable in their mountainous
beings that rough bamboo huts with rough-hewn fences and
long-bearded sages as in T'ang Dynasty scrolls had
   blinked into existence and then
blinked out again
like the silent breathing of frogs —

inside the smoke cursive love letters had been
written, as this poem is being written, during a full moon,
making little or less sense than this poem,
but heading straight for the heart as this
poem and all poems intend,
and lovers' eyes filled with tears, and lovers'
pens overflowed with replies now lost, repeated
indecipherably by the swoop of hovering cuckoos and
    arcs of various flying squirrels,
and old people became younger, and
young people became older as usual, and

each transition from one form to another, from
one moment to another inside that
smoke had tiny gold stairways connecting,
tiny gold sunset-viewing vistas, a
    curved gold bridge over a golden stream
        to watch sunrays get
           shorter then
    shrink into deep golden
dark until morning.

And at the center of the green smoke was God's inaudible
 Voice, to which all other sound is
noise, all other considerations and
    contemplations are
finicky physical motions, all other time/space realities
are the flutter of inconsiderable wings,

a Voice not of wind or woe, blue sky or fire,
nor of anything heard or anything

unheard in the seven worlds and
heavens,

God's Voice articulating
     gold,

and the alchemist's gray head grew gradually
  young again,
and in his moist eyes he's
knocking on his beloved's door, his
arms full of gold roses.

The door
opens and his heart

bursts into bloom
at that vision.

                                          6/1

ON THIS SIDE OF SLEEP

for Geoffrey Manaugh

On this side of sleep, where my
  back garden extends its bamboo-fenced
weedy rectangle of miniature woodland
    out to a garbage-can back alley,
where a real city materializes like a pop-up of
  buildings, tenements with people in them
on that side of sleep at this hour (5A.M.),
skyscrapers with thin bluish light seeping
  in through 40th floor venetian blinds,

where wild hills and valleys outstretch and yawn
    connecting to other states and finally
sand themselves down to a fine powder in the froth of
    east coast or west coast seas,
here on the side of the
very seas themselves, watery
    reversals of sky, sea-creatures
      fiercer than mythic beasts
snapping sharp jaws fully awake in
black waters miles below,

on this side of sleep of
other continents distant in the
  dark or in sunlight where people order
ice-cream in another language, or
    politely inquire the

    price of a broom using different words,
make love in secret rooms whispering in
French, Hungarian or Chinese,

on this side of sleep I find myself in now
where people are born from a sperm-drop hitting an
    egg-wall and burrowing in,
where people hit the implacable shell of death and go
    through it, and are then lowered
        gently down into fertile earth
to sleep in its blue/green rotating egg
          until trumpet-time
            sweeps them awake,

this earth-egg circling a fiery sun that itself
   circles only
God-knows-what in space going only
God-knows-where
  at astronomical speeds,

One clear Eye on all of us at once,

on this side of sleep where I hear birds at dawn making
poems simpler but far more intricate than this one,
where people plan escapades less melodious than those
performed in dream, less
   slow-motioned or sped up
  with obvious symbolic meaning,

there where a door of ice opens on antlered
   figures in white smoke remembering the

    minutest details of our childhoods, or
clouds open up on the inner consciousness of an eagle
    gliding high in the
        sky through our own eyes,

while on this side of sleep
murderers walk freely among their victims,
tyrants dine on squab and white wine,
trucks start up in the dawn,

the usual miracles are performed,
and I sit on my bed with my
two feet planted firmly on the floor
to write this.

                                                          6/4

POSSIBLE ANGELS

I sleep on the floor on a thin mat in my
   own house tonight due to
two out-of-town guests on their way
to sell clothes and books at a yearly bazaar
then head north to Rhode Island. They

are human beings, feet with toes, hands, hearts with
secret histories inside, eyes like mine
that look out on the world from
deep intelligence and sky-like consciousness.

They do not tuck great wings underneath them
to sleep, though they might be angels, they
might have been angels all along.
They came
  out of the unseen and go
    back into the unseen again
when they go. Where they go
  I have no idea, it could be Tahiti, it
    could be the arctic — Oh God,
carry them there in Your arms and care for their
precious souls as You care for mine. I

may not see them again when they go, they
may not see me, they go back into the great
concave globe of their lives and
  it closes behind them
    to my view. I go back into

mine. Like turtles, each
   into our shell, cared for by
      You. Now however

they are asleep, one on his back with his
mouth open, one on his side, completely
at ease and at peace in the
   populated solitude of their sleep. My

wife and two children are also asleep, and they
do not tuck great wings underneath them
   to sleep, though they too may have been
angels all along in human form. They certainly
   scatter enough light. They certainly
open the way enough for themselves and
   others to enter. Their
      words are sweet. Their

eyes, black, brown, blue, hazel, black central
pupils, hearts of apertures in space,
receptor-dishes for the multi-million
      variations of light cast by
form and non-form in
   this world.

I sleep on the floor in my own house tonight.
I do not tuck wings underneath me
   to do so.

Good night.

6/8

ADVICE IN OUR SLEEP

It seems the poetry of awakening's become
    a poetry of sleep.
Here are green banks covered with
    monarch butterflies,
clouds to the ground you set
    foot on and ride to the
        bluest Empyrean.

But crack open a single wink of sleep like a
    fortune cookie and you'll get
aphorisms about enlightenment enough to
    dazzle you awake at least for
        ten millennia.
Such as: *"If you rest your head on*
    cold tracks,
you'll hear the train coming!"

Or, *"A bird singing in a lightening*
    dawn sky
        is not just being temperamental."

Or, *"Say Allah, and the rest will*
be easy."

                                                         6/15

RUBY RED

A cry goes out across the
   curvature of the earth:
"Ruby red! Ruby red!"
Who uttered such a cry, no one
   knows, but the cock struts
     more robustly, sea waves
crash with a louder crack,
clouds bunch then disperse with a jerk,
light almost blinks, then
   spreads brighter sheets of
     incandescence to the
four edges of awakening and its
   aftermath: Sage advice.
All from two words.
Substitute *"ruby red"* with *"daily bread,"*
or *"Flight from pelicans light as feathers,"*
or put in a recipe for strudel — the
effect would be quite different.

"Ruby red! Ruby red!"
Double chins disappear, families
   reunite, squirrels
square dance in the trees, dawns all across the
globe come up simultaneously.
Breathing becomes deeper and more
   rhythmic. Sandstone
shines.

A little lady in Wisconsin at her
   windowsill with
      chin in hands was thought for a
while to be the utterer of this cry,
for no reason. She often was heard to
say, *"All that glitters is gold,"* or
"Diamonds are a pearl's best friend,"
but even in her dreamier states, after
   putting in a full day at the
      yarn factory, she never said
"Ruby red."

A child sitting by a brook was the
   next choice. He was
handsome as a small horse, his black hair
and face glistened, he looked in the
bouncing waters and yelled
"Turquoise tornados! Azure assurances!"
But never *"Ruby red!"*

In some states
those with something more than a purely
  political bent are still
    seeking the answer to this
      enigma.
Others, more seasoned, just smile, almost
  knowingly. They've
    been there. Now their
vistas are longer, and include more
inconsistencies and incongruities without
wrenching their whole

nervous systems out of whack.
A few *"Ruby reds"* don't
rearrange their neat cosmologies.

They've rested assured.

They hear the distant cuckoo.

6/23

BEHIND EVERY PATCH OF SUNLIGHT

1

Behind every patch of sunlight
   there's a group of singers in a circle
whose voices make sounds even
   brighter rays shoot from.

Behind every object in the sun's path
there's a shadow, and in that
   shadow a dark kingdom lies
where a silent chorus standing in a line
makes no sound, with heavy lids and
   trembling chins.

Forests thrive in the interstices,
wild animals roam in the atmosphere,
doorways may lead to another room
or be a sheer drop down a
   glassy canyon of sighs and whispers,
an opening onto more than a room,
a green glade of absolute quiet
where a blue stream glides as
   softly as thought through
      tall grasses and flowery meadows.

The furniture in a room may look
   solid and unoccupied, but be, in fact,
part of a transparent assembly

filled by gloriously seated hierarchies of
  angels who've somehow
    folded their wings so there's
  level upon level of incandescence
    rising into the highest heaven.

A cloud may float through a room
which is an angelic heartbeat making itself
known in the midst of routine life,
and routine life itself, which may look so
normal and humdrum
may be, in fact, a two-way mirror in
  space that is full of fantastic
happenings and miraculous occurrences,
beasts from the deeps fastening red eyes on our
proceedings, flying pterodactyls out of
time from antiquity's nethermost skies
swooping through our conversations to impart a
sense of historical deja vue, or
the sudden realization of how truly
ancient every encounter is, how
hallowed with drenched timelessness
every utterance is, uttered aloud or
silently to oneself, or
expressed with all the added tone of
  glistening eye and roll of tongue
and facial sweetness
    to someone else.

The world we see and live in
shifts and breathes and turns

tragedy into a festival and drops a
festival down through a gap in the
earth suddenly to the sound of
dark chimes of doom.

Sorrows may be sung into
   jubilation, melancholy into
dawn birdsong and the splash of
continuous fountains.

2

What world do we live in, I'm
   always interested to know? I
don't like to hold out for this one, with its
   drowning prospects and a
future that every day seems more a
   matter of electricity than reality.

Already our faces go through a tissue-thin
membrane in space to come out in a
   brilliant courtyard with
arches in all directions and someone
   playing a lute.
While the backs of us, like the
   back of the moon, bathe in
darkness.

We handle things while we've the strength,
let them go as we also are let go

into the pouring stream.

Our loves are like leaping deer,
   arcs from a darkness into a
     darkness, but such sleek
animal forms in the little light between!

Somehow, on this earthly floor, in these
earthly rooms, under these
   earthly roofs, we know we're actually
God's ants following a scented trail back to the
hill, or on an exploratory adventure that may end
at a picnic, or a sink, our little
   feelers twitching, our eyes
peering out for foothold.

We are creatures of light, encouraged by
    light, nourished by its
immaterial substance, carried to the
tomb in its arms.

We've lived in the world we've lived in.

Let love be its leavening.

                                                               6/24-25

RÉSUMÉ

1

A little dumb, a little smart,
  he feels all used up.

A little dull, a little sharp,
  his heart's a mountain range on fire.

The world's upside-down inside him,
  or right side up outside him.

He's right on target
  or way off in cloud-land.

He's a lark full of rye grass
  or a barren field of tares beaten down.

The sun can scorch a big one on him.
Rain can fall on his head and leave a hole.

He's been in love, he could be in
  love now, how does he know?

He remembers hotter days, wilder blizzards.
Does that mean the days now are dog days?

Dogs bite him. Cats ignore him.
  Is there dirt somewhere

where he can lie down?

He plays dead, but that's no good.
He plays alive, but no one's fooled.

The days lengthen way past him.
The past lengthens way behind him.

He burns the moment up.

The moment's like a huge ball bearing
   in a greased groove, glittering silver.

He moves it along with one hand
while the other clutches his neck, or
   signs checks.

He's all shy, he's all gregarious, his
   skeleton falls out the
      closet of his flesh.

I'd say this is a riddle, but it isn't.
We all know the answer, and it
   weighs upon us.

He's six foot three, he's five foot two.
He's so short you might overlook him.

He's as eloquent as a fool.

I quit. The

birds know better than I do
   what his name is, place of
origin, destination.

He's a sly fox. He's as
   simple as a clothespin.

The human condition's got
   nothing on him.

2

A man with the head of a duck
walked into a French Restaurant...

a man with fire hose legs
tried to straddle a burning department store...

two men in identical bowler hats and
faces of meat grinders went sailing...

a man and a woman with bodies of
ceramic cookie jars settled down on
   green towels at the beach...

two women with identical noses and overbites,
but not twins, and one green
   eye and one blue eye, sat on a log...

a lady with the face of a best selling

    novel walked naked into
       the living room one
    evening while we were watching
       television...

a man with hands of grand pianos was
running along the highway shouting:
"Rhapsody in Blue, Rhapsody in Black!"

3

Man is a fetid gunnysack with legs
unless he be brought to life with light.

He's a long tunnel full of scary
   thoughts and oncoming trains
unless he finds in the center of the pearl of his heart
the story of new moonlight and the
essential source of things, and scans
with his own eyes the
miraculous permutations
   in all their momentary
manifest perfection.

The story steps out of the pages of books and
   dry desert lips
of God's anointing of some men as prophets
   with a community of believers,
and some as rejectors, vicious as
   cockroaches in history's filthy kitchen.

And how the story, so universal, encroaches
on all of us until it can be seen to
represent us as well
  in whatever environment.

Pull aside the tent flaps
  and there we are!

Oh, pull them aside!

The story of desert derring-do
become intimately ours.

And we made more
  animate by it.

7/11-13

MOTHER TONGUE

I would love to write these poems in
   another language.
The stars of other heavens might look
   down on them. Like
Becket, Conrad, Nabokov, or more
   recently Brodsky, unreeling strings of
mysterious foreign syllables, letting the
imagery float like foam on distant seas,
   etcetera... Folding into

literatures other than American or English, but
   then running into obstacles not
     encountered here. I'm

writing in a Chinese notebook, black
   cover with red binding and
blue-lined paper definitely set up for
   English, but suppose I was
writing in Chinese, and had to be
   careful I wasn't painting subversive
images with my inky brush, or writing in a tone
  inimical to tyranny, and therefore
   subject to punishment, or
even getting more aggressively ignored than in
   America. Flattened with a
steamroller, paraded through streets in a
  dunce cap, with the bold characters for
   "traitor" in a poster around my

son-to-be severed neck.

In Spanish I might be in the same bin of
   ripe fruits as you'd find Neruda,
or more darkly dangerous modern poets in
    Spanish who might talk about
revolution, dead imperialists with
   dollars stuffed in their
      mouths, or giant
surrealist armadillos spouting
    Socialist slogans.

Writing in French would mean perhaps greater abstraction,
   language of nuance, language of
    vowel-sounds clipped off by the
  most fragile of consonants, language of
roses, purple, cities bathed in
    bronze, or
  grotesque faces along rooftops under
     thunderous skies. Musical
dreams from a Gallic source, absurd
  propaganda in language
for the winged giraffes of
    the unconscious.

Arabic would usher me into the mysteries,
  golden globes of meaning hanging on boughs of
    fig or olive over rough garden walls
or in blasted fields of righteous anger and
    nostalgia, pearlescent miniatures
in stamped silver settings of a

    language going all the way
        back to Adam.

But I write these poor poems in English, always
   elusive, words jostling for
     positions of importance, spiritual
light coming through with
    difficulty, since the King James version and
      centuries of imitations of Shakespeare,
until the distillations of Dickinson and the
broad Whitmanian vistas, are our only
       forebears.

But the evergreen birds of American English hatch in my heart
and their wings turn gold in my throat, and
   occasionally fly out in
   beams of light from my lips,
light wings toppling the paper towers of commerce,
 heading toward clouds of
   a technicolor radiance,

language of my childhood, in whose native tongue

my next-to-last words, God willing, will be
    framed.

                              7/13

I SPY A LAND BEYOND CLOUDS

I spy a land beyond clouds
   lying just past my breath
where two suns shine,
twelve moons revolve, bright
green rivers rise and fall,
  trees fill with birds of light,
    the air's edible, its
      scents as sweet as
love-thoughts, water as
  refreshing as thirst is
    despairing, God's Hand
visible over all.

I want to dwell there. I must have
dwelt there before. My
  eyes don't see it, but my
heart sees it, and to
  step out onto it should be
    easy — but it's
      not.

It takes a moment whose superstructure
  of angels announces itself clearly
    or we so totally trust its
availability that the step is
  of a foolhardiness only wisdom
    dares, and then it's
there, it's totally there,

strung out like bridge-lights from our
    selves across watery
        darkness into the

next world's nearness.

                                        7/14

ONE OF US

In memoriam Jesse Adler

One of us has just died. Familiar features
   now unmoving. Eyelids
unfluttering. Nose and mouth no longer
air conduits, speech conduits.
The body now like a frosting of light about to
   dissolve around the
     invisible soul, the hard
bony part emerging. Foam
thrown onto beach from terrible
sea-depths, glistening a moment in the
   sun, then
     vanishing completely away.

I knew him and felt his warmth,
exchanged a few words, his being
lingered a little in my mind. He
   moved among living things.
Now he lies still while restless ones
shift around him, until we too, one
   by one, lie still, and the

sky stares out from itself above us,
and clouds making variable forms above us
take the place of facial expressions,
and dark night with its
   little creatures who come out

    at night to hunt
takes the place of our innermost thoughts and
    distracted thought-flights,
and the long day with its arcing solar
   light and heat
takes the place of heart's warmth and natural
   body-warmth,

and a shattering canopy of angels, silvery and
   silent, comes across us and
all around us, and we lie like an echo

after its sound has been made, pause after
utterance, God's Majestic Motions
   having been made through us, God's
utter silence now so eloquently

lying still
inside us.

                                                             7/16

SONG FOR THE MILLENNIUM

The millenniums call out to each other
   across the great divide of time
like a mass of people who arrive at a
   shore and call out to the waves
or to distant fishing boats who
     can't hear them.

Each time a century starts
it's an edge.
Enchanted scissors cut time a neat slice
and the start of the year
takes place as if on ice over deep water,
revellers dangerously drunk and disorderly
cut off from the previous people in suddenly
   out-of-fashion clothes and quirks
     and ways of thinking
separated from the forward flow of time
as stiff as mannikins
locked in department store show windows
   that've gone out of business.

But a giant millennial angel bright as polished pewter
with sweeping yellow wings and face of
   lunar innocence
pulls by and stretches all the way from the
anguished souls of the former century
to the souls, born and unborn, of the next
who somehow think they're

    free of time and responsiblity and the
        legacy of the last century

and this delectable angel deftly puts in their eyes
a supernal radiance that shows
the one heart of humankind
has a single song to sing
to a single Listener

however it may be perceived by the
    eight billion crowding the

planet at the time.

                                                            7/19

FROM WHERE I SIT

From where I sit I see
a canyon wall facing me.

Polished to mirror shine, it
reflects the whole world back to me.

Because it's the canyon of my goal
through which the River of Satisfaction flows

it also reflects my poor life
back to me,

so I can see
in its clear surface all the

murky surfaces juxtaposed that are
particular to me.

Above the canyon wall is a shower of
lights that explodes continually

and I set out from here with deep
intention to proceed

unceremoniously.

O single Lord of Intentions and Destinations,
bring me in and guide me!

7/21

LITTLE BLACK FLY ON THE WALL

The little black fly on the wall doesn't stop to
   think what he knows, those
     multiple eyes are enough. God's
sight through them shows him the world.

Birds don't think, *"Fly or soar as I*
   might, I'm only a bird in a
     bird's world, one
eye on each side of my head, my
     limited universe not
        enough!"

The worm in the sod blind as
death, pushing through darkness it may not
see, does it think
"I wish I could stand
on two legs in a drawing room and sip
tea as I listen to someone
  at a spinet play Mozart"?

Enclosed in the world, we enclose the world, and
it's enclosed inside us until
we open. We'll bump into
   every wall until we
go from world to
   Creator of world, Who's
given us our world apparatus and sensitive
contraption for grasping the world, and

if we sight along His
  cross-hairs in the
    Unseen we should
      see Him originating this
display.

He who
  creates us as we
    go.

Fly, bird and worm, and
man, hearts on the
    optical throne.

Light
filling us to the brim.

In which to
see Him.

                        7/22

I DON'T KNOW

I don't know, my dear ones, my
hornets asleep in hornet heaven, gnats and
beetles in the air and in the grass,
sometimes earth life is too much for me,
ache in the neck, arm sore, head a
   confused bramble, eyes just
optic balls in physical sockets,
the ceiling fan circulating what
    little air there is, while
past imagined velvet drapes of royal
   red or funereal black or ocean blue
the real world lies, but I'm not

in it, rolling on a beach like a
   deeply intoned vowel, or
circulating with air currents among
   wide cactus blades, wheeling with
high hawks. Imagination has its
limits. Actions are the miracles. I
    should have given my jacket to that
shivering black man in the morning mist who had
   a savage, hungry look, recalling
Arthur Rimbaud's phrase,
"Charity is the key! This proves I've been
      dreaming!"

Yet, O earth, leaden, heavy, tending deeply toward
inertia, the body's roller coaster support for

the spirit's excitement gradually
    eroding, another source of
momentary strength from God alone
    fervently hoped for.

Penguins dive off iceberg cliffs in full
    dinner dress.
Camels stand in silhouette against scorching dunes.
Almost totally insubstantial alive
    entities float in outer space between
        solitary celestial bodies like
        echoes, twisting as slowly as
    kelp ribbons along the sea bottom.

I would be a wide window, a complete
    slave. I would be

what God wants me to be. Quiet or
rambunctious.

A raindrop or a flood.

I would have the Name of God
reverberate in my blood.

7/24

IN THIS WORLD OF MULTIPLE SOLITARIES

Sailing alone on a green sea,
sitting alone under a green tree,

hammering alone at the edge of night
trying to penetrate anthracite,

walking alone in a strange town,
alone in woods, all crows flown,

silent as paint, silvery, alone,
solitary nugget whose light has shown

and shines out periodically now,
secret as the obvious meaning of Tao,

only furtively showing its face,
true heart solitary in its place,

shimmering images, rivering bright,
poignant soul of us, in God's sight,

on earth day to day, night after night,
on fields of actions in broad daylight

gazing at cloud-tufts passing in sky
through our life's orb, our soul's eye

— observer of innermost outer things —

seeing what Allah in His wisdom brings

to our door to grieve through or befriend,
in this world where multiple solitaries end.

7/25

GREENNESS OF MY GARDEN

I want to dissolve into the greenness of my garden,
I want to go down into the greenness and be gone.

The grass and growing leaves and ribbons of
   green, green atmospheres around
fragile tendrils and threads as they
reach into air for sustenance or
   handhold, slow and gradual, but

intrepidly growing, incessantly patient
Job, sweet green of my garden! Sweet,
   sweet greenness I would
disappear into, pop as a
   bubble without trace, take on the
green of the garden as I lose my own,

reappear without blink as a green panorama of
each inch full of green life, each
tiny plot on earth with deeps and creatures,
green leaves overhanging meeting long green blades upreaching,
stems ending in clusters of green bulbs flowering,

bursts of light and dark enclosed in the
green globe of my garden. The
green globe of my garden I would go
into and be gone.

                                                                 7/27

OUT IN THE LONGITUDINAL AIR

Out in the longitudinal air,
in miraculous latitudes of light and
    birdsong, nearing dusk,
consciousness stretched between east and west,
cheek on fist, sitting in my chair,
birds all around, bus sound, voices,
the end of a perfect day drawing near, each
    leaf distinct, each molecular cell,
bird twortle and liquid squeak, I
    fling myself out, or rather, let myself
    down and down into silence,
deeper than did ever plummet sound, or
    rather, letting outer sound and
inner soundlessness touch at the margins,
those frizzled edges where opposites meet, in the
        greater air.

Here, on torchlit horizons, giants stride,
    uprooting trees with one swipe, throwing
ten-ton oxen over their shoulders, bellowing like
    God. Or so we think. God is another
        sound.

And here great expeditions go in search of silk
or channels to the Orient. Swagger and
    slide through great waves in the
dwindling dark. Or so it seems. The light
rising on more seas and more horizons, with

    no land near.

But also here, in the extended air, there are
single souls whose lakes have been ladled with
gold, whose light has ignited and burns
clear. Their faces are torches and their
hearts beat without fear

in this air.

                                                              7/27

IT'S HARD IF YOU'RE DEAD

It's hard if you're dead
   to sip clear liquid,
it's hard if you're dead
   to run down the street,
it's hard if you're dead
   to deny The Divinity
that's shaped our ends
    as well as our feet.

Once dead it's over,
the eternal question,
once dead it's over,
the mortgage being due,
once dead it's over,
the worry about whether
to worship God
if the sky is blue.

When we're stretched out flat
the debate is over,
when our hands are folded
the results are clear,
when our eyelids are closed
the gnawing doubts
are dissipated about
why we're here.

The light will bathe us

from head to foot,
the light will bathe us
and make us still.
New eyes replace
the ones now useless
to see the truth
come down the hill.

Establish our beings
once and for all,
establish our beings
in heavenly realms
while our sensual bodies,
now not so sensual,
are solemnly buried
under the elms.

It's a wondrous day
when we see the light,
it's a wondrous day
when it opens our hearts.
We don't get much chance
in this illusory world
to notice how completely
it floods our parts

and brings to life
what once was dead,
as when we're dead
we'll see for sure
and see God's Face

if what we're left with
is at least in some part
completely pure.

Once dead, the dithering
flattering falseness
that dogged our steps
will be dead and gone,
while once we're dead
our true reality
will be brought to life
in eternal dawn.

Truth will live
and falsehood die
when we lie down
as good as dead,
no longer running
all around
to prove we've something
inside our head.

The landscape stretches
all around us
as we're stretched out
in angelic arms.
The sky arrives
with all its legions
to show us its
otherworldly charms.

A trumpet sound
obliterates silence
and makes the orchestra
of light resound,
and at that moment
in all eternity
the truth of our being
will be found.

May God have mercy
on every one of us
alive now and listening
to dawn's birdsong.
This life flows by
so terribly short,
but the river it's in
is long.

Hey!

The river it's in
is long.

7/29

I END MY SONG

*"The wise man laid his head back on an egg
and his toe tapped a tiny door open in heaven."*

I heard these words as I
   contemplated going back to sleep.
I saw clouds in a blue sky.
It is just past dawn, and somewhere on this
   planet a Great Blue Heron
     extends its wings and swoops
down onto a glistening fish just below the
twinkling surface of a lake.

A piano sits underwater. A
   woman in seaweed dress sits
down on a conch bench to play an
aquamarine sonata.

Deer with antlers in the shapes of
   fantastic architecture
prance across detailed tundra, endlessly
   tiny wildflowers every
     color of the rainbow
embroidering the natural tapestry.

Somewhere a ship's captain is sobering up
as the ship goes down, all hands
on deck. He prays to God for the
first time in twenty years. Gates as wide as the

   entire Atlantic open up to let them
      enter. They're
         given a celestial reception.
Light falls over their eyes.

Not everyone will see when the time for perfect
vision arrives. We can
only pray to be among the pure-sighted ones.

Many small animals
   gather around their mothers
      at the first snow.

We bid farewell to the present moment each
     time we breathe out.

We lie down sweetly in the present moment as we
inhale its palpable sweetness.

Our heartbeats provide the kick drum.

An alligator slitheriness keeps our
      intellects strong.

I end my song.

                                                         8/1

TOM-TOM

No one has ever written a poem from
  pre-birth or post-death,
maybe they've fantasized, even imagining the
    slide down birth canal or
Lethean slip in black canoe over death's waters,
but we haven't ever had any direct messages from
  either quarter, those
    domains self-enclosed,
full of hopeful joys and terrors,

the pinkish, close, all-embracing entry via
    womanish womb, nuclear
  thrust into daylight from soft night,
sights and sounds abruptly intensified,
acrid taste of oxygen in lungs first time,

the Zen *"Ah!"*, or even more forceful
"Ahah!" experience, with multiple
repeats either more or less Zen afterwards
  as little fists clench around whatever's
    available, where before
outer-space free-fall was the norm,

and little lips clench around a milky
    nipple, becoming a
syrupy fleshly world we must now
    fight through to the death — unless it's a
      lifeless rubbery one.

And death, that gory picture postcard
from nowhere, we imagine ourselves in
all kinds of grotesque situations in this
giant material-world-womb we
get thrust out of into
death's next chamber, under blocks of
concrete or hot lava in plane crash
wreckage on ice-bound mountaintop or
deep undersea, eyeblinks on deathbed or
final heartbreak while walking, some

quick knock-knocking on our mortal door, or a
gradual reverberation hammering our
visceral wood to leave this world,

and we go through without real
resistance at both
    critical moments,

our death agreement the parchment we've
been waiting to sign on the
dotted line from moment of birth all our
  days deep inside our skin,
    signed with a
  flourish or with weak
delirious hand, pencil forcefully inserted,

then the spirit ride begins, cloud-wheels
    start turning,
raucous or close-harmony singing starts up,

the body is moved without our assistance or
intervention, we lie in the boat of our
own flesh and bones for the
   long journey, each of our actions
      tattooed indelibly
         upon us,

and go to where we came from but in an
opposite direction, and we've got
vivid reports from prophets about what to
expect there, but no one's ever
totally been and then physically come back to
confirm, which is as it should be, in

God's good wisdom, our heart-space
expand to that blind vision in this
life, to see the antlers of its
celestial life cast shadows on our
forest, dark stars at a distance
delineate our human constellation as in
pre-birth and post-death, with

utter faith our spirit's
   eyes blink open
to see in this
     world what
can't be seen
   though our
heartbeats become its
     inalienable
tom-tom.

                                                                         8/3

KEEPING WATCH

The dew outside falls through the sky on its
   way to adorn the necks of
     grass blades.

Particles of dust fall from the ceiling of my room
   into my sleeping mouth as well as
     onto the zither strings.
They reverberate slightly at the moment of impact.

A bird who has its own soul and not the
soul of a transgressed
   town mayor reincarnated onto a
     lower if more musical rung
fluffs its breast feathers with its beak in
   search of the itch or for
     sheer beauty's sake.

The furniture in the room settles minutely into the
carpet in the dark room, its wood
   thickening as it absorbs the
     moisture of summer humidity.

A slug, glistening prettily in the full
     moonlight on the walk
doesn't think so much as sluggishly notice
a difference in texture as it
slides off asphalt onto wet night grass.

A star explodes from deep within its core, and the
   debris flies up for miles into
      frictionless space, the star's
         glow deepening. The
space around it becomes illuminated for awhile
   until the debris cools down.

Many beautiful picture books lie against each
other in my room bereft of shelf space,
Persian Painting leaning against *Mecca* leaning against
   Bedouin leaning against *The History of Invention*
     leaning against *Sunrise of Power*.

My tired eyes burn for lack of sleep as the
mockingbird outside stretches its
territory effortlessly by sounding like
   every bird possible within maybe a few thousand
      yard's radius.

God's world revolves and falls and gyrates
effortlessly in different dimensions in
    space and time, as I
lie back on my bed for a few more
hours of sleep

having kept watch over a few tiny
   moments of its existence
in a few square meters of its
     life.

8/5

EVERYTHING WAS AS IT SHOULD BE

Everything was as it should be,
  square pegs were driven into round holes,
bicycles were put out to pasture,
the twain never met, he could
go to sleep content
and wake up in a reasonable world.

Only, as soon as he slept,
round holes ejected their pegs,
people started telling the truth,
oldsters in city parks began dancing,
one lion actually laid down next to a lamb,
both feet turned out to be the best one
and were immediately put forward,
the sky, instead of falling, actually
  rose a few inches, you could
poke your head through and see some of the
lower workings of the universe,
not completely reasonable (black became
white, all horses became
  wingéd, that sort of thing)
but eminently workable.

Crazy Jane stopped talking to spiders.

I'm not sure how long this all lasted,
but as soon as he came round again
square pegs were wedged firmly in

  round holes, people said
anything that came into their heads, the more
  outlandish the better,
and the lion bent over and bit off the lamb's
 poor fleecy head as was expected.

What was unexpected had been so refreshing
to everyone but him.

Birds flew from tree to tree.

He smiled approvingly.

              8/7

UPWARD SHOWER OF PURE SOUND

There's a sound in the air that starts as a tiny note,
but if you follow it it opens into a full-blown symphony,
it's a thin tone floating on atmosphere, almost
   negligible among the bangs and
      clanks of everyday,
but as our ears tilt in its direction they discern
strands and threads like rivers
branching and becoming full,
flowing between houses and hillsides and heading toward the
   open sea,

the sound that began as one near note, a vague
   cluster of reverberations off to the
      side it seems of conversation or the
clinking of glasses or silverware,
slowly and with gradual accumulation
becomes a dense but transparent
texture of tones, deep and high, harmonic and
   dissonant, harps and trumpets, voices
floating throughout each dot of music, dividing
   at a note and reuniting on the
other side, voices of more than
human, clear as mountain air and pale turquoise sky,
drawing us forward until we become

listening canoes of light shooting forward on its
   waves which buoy us up exquisitely, pull us out
toward ever-widening sound, unweave our own

perplexities, draw our own threads out and re-
   weave them on rivers of multiple tone,

blue-silver cloud up ahead, clear
   foghorn sonorous as an undersea groan
up ahead, and the
sound finally opens out
as a vast cloud hovering over oceanic waves,
a vast held chord of rainbow richness
hovering over the ocean, dark waters heaving and
rolling underneath, waters
rushing to crash on solid shore, the
high element of sound as if

listened to by God alone in the whole universe
standing still in the air above the ocean

in a never-ending
upward shower of pure sound.

8/8

FABLES WRITTEN DURING A FLIGHT FROM CHICAGO TO PHILADELPHIA

1

A tree wanted to be a bird.
It stood in the forest and told all its neighbors
   about its longing to fly.
The other trees just shook their leaves at him
    derisively.
Whenever a bird landed on its branches it would
ask how it feels to fly.
It would tell the bird about its desire, but
   birds don't have much time for lengthy
     conversations.

Time passed the way time passes for trees.
Rings would be added around its central core.
Generations of squirrels and other small mammals
lived and died in its trunks and branches.
Insects mated on its
   vertical and horizontal surfaces.
Seasons came and went.

Even as a very old tree it never gave up its
   desire to be a bird.

Curiously, none of the birds in that forest
   ever wanted to be a tree.

2

An ant struck out on its own and
decided to build a giant palace on a
    rock.
It left the formic acid trail and
found a large rock next to a stream.
It had a beautiful view of the water on one
   side and a gorge and hillside on the
      other.
It was isolated without being desolate.
It got the early morning sun and was
shady in the heat of the afternoon.
At night he could sit on the rock in full view
    of the moon.
It was perfect.

The ant accumulated building materials and
    set to work.
Bits of gravel and shale, portions of
   dry leaves, ends of twigs.
He built a beautiful palace and went into it
to try it out.
He pushed a few of the gravel grains around until he
   had a perfect terrace for viewing the
     landscape, or sitting out under the
       stars in the moonlight.

The only thing he lacked was a queen.
But the view continues to excite him.

3

A flying saucer landed among some Australian
   Aborigines, ones who had
refused levis and denim shirts and
continued to walk around in the pitiless sun
     naked.
It seems they had been expecting it.

When the Martians slithered out of the saucer
the Aborigines entered into telepathic communication with them
as easily as a ray of sunlight enters a crevice.
They tossed off some humorous remarks,
    joked around a little in little
      haiku bursts, then went into
deeper modes of thought.

Soon they were jointly appreciating circles and
triangles, luminous loops and the
   rising and setting of worlds.

Around the campfire that night you could
hardly distinguish between the body-painted
   Aborigines and their
     body-painted guests.

Their song echoed in the dusty valley.

4

"There is never an empty space in the universe,"
    the scholar thought, seated
        among his books.
"Allah's secret voice permeates everywhere, leaving
    no stone untuned, no tome
        entombed, no tomb undone. No
            stone unturned..."
He liked to string his thoughts out across a
little abyss of associations from time to time.

"There is never an empty space..."
He gazed into space for a moment, leaving his
    thoughts blank, formless and
        nameless.

There was no word for the state he was in.
In the space available to him there appeared
a tiny calligraphic figure, the
    name of Allah in perfect delicate script.
Around it was a halo the color of ripe plum.
It shone as smooth as ivory. It
suddenly split apart and in a
split second the scholar found himself
    among his books thinking

"There is never an empty space in the universe...
Allah's secret voice permeates everywhere..."

                                        8/11

THE RAIN HAS BEEN FALLING

The rain has been falling
  a hundred nights and a hundred days
and things are melting, the bicycle is
   melting, sliding down from its rigid
     form into the mud under its wheels,
and all along the curvature of this
  part of the world things are leaving their
silhouette shapes to go
  back into liquid, houses are
sinking into their foundations, harps in
  attics, grand pianos going
down into sonorous lumps, trucks and cars
  elongating then stretching like
taffy, picket fences slanting then
sinking down, brick walls like furrowing
brows which thought they would
  last forever become worms of
their former selves then
sink down without trace,

  then giant buildings with faces of glass
in the endless rain become blurry expressions
then faces of malleable melancholy,
then tragic groans, then
   nothing at all, and finally
people like melting wax dissolve into
   dreamlike shapes with their
     hands on their cheeks, their

      mouths awry, their
eyes beseeching the God of this rain of a
hundred years in a single moment, the

water falling from a watery heaven, dissolving
everything in its path toward an
    ocean of purity and dissolution,

each thing calling out the name of its Lord in the
sigh of its molecules

as the slurping rain continues to
    fall from the sky.

                                                             8/13

NEW YORK

I'm in New York but I don't speak a
    word of English, I've
never eaten western food, and I was
only away from my home village once when I was
a child of five, for one night, with my
uncle on the opposite hillside across the
      wide valley.

I watch the people go by from a small
bench I have found on the sidewalk.
There are more varieties of human being here even than
the fantastic figures of my dreams, with more
varied and peculiar expressions on their faces,
inflections in their voices, strange
    words on their lips and then
      afloat in the air between them as they
        walk.

I am seeing life with new eyes.

I am hearing life with new ears.

I might as well be a cricket in a
    world of butterflies, or a
      bird in a world of
hairy mammals.

Cars and trucks rattle by.

The sun slides its golden silks down the
   sides of buildings until the
     dusk takes over,
the same dark that fell with a billion
   twinkles every night in my

village in *The Land of the Clear-Headed Ones,*

The Land of the First Race. The

Land of Twelve-Star Human Beings.

                                                                  8/20

I WAKE UP WITH A START

I wake up with a start
with my head up out of the swamp.

I wake up with a start
just after zebra dust has settled.

I wake up with a start
and nothing new in my bedroom but air.

I wake up with a start —
the same liars and thieves running world
    governments.

I wake up with a start
pregnant with poetry. Who entered me in the
    night?

I wake up with a start
and my waking consciousness continues where it
    left off.

I wake up with a start
in God's universe facing the Creator as always.

                                                                       8/22

PYTHIAN THE ANGLER

Pythian the Angler disappeared in the pearly waves
looking for the perfect catch.
Clouds covered the sun with gray gauze
and sea water stung his cheeks.

Orpheus rode the waves with only his
   head above water.

Phinneas the goldsmith polished the ewer's side
until the whole world reflected in its bulge.
He polished almost unto madness
  for the world is not a golden place
    but he longed to behold it so.

Lazbeth played the harp with her long fingernails.
She hardly brushed the strings, for she
   wanted the sound of earth, sea and sky
to emerge from things and mingle in her
     music.
She sat on the same mountaintop year after year
as creatures and stones gamboled and
   danced around her.

The earth is a singular place full of
   dark magnificence.
A deep green hill with a deep green
forest on top
in which the creatures of night

peep their faces out only on special occasions.

Each of us seeks perfection.

There is no death among strangers.

Earth is a pinpoint of light among
    billions of galaxies.

                                                          8/22

KING OF LOCUSTS

The King of Locusts called a meeting of the
   Apocalyptic creatures
     together: There was the President of
Rivers of Blood, the Ambassador of Rainfalls of
   Frogs, the CEO of Sulphurous
     Smoke from the East, various
Plagues, AIDS, cancer, the common cold, the
Demon of Mediocrity, the Infernal
   Angel of Blandness — they had
all convened at the Crater of the Dead
to work out the timetable for the End of the
World.

The minutes from the last meeting were
read out, which took an entire
   millennium. Tablets were
brought in and deciphered, mummies
resurrected and commanded to
speak, poets labeled "mad" in their
own time, in whose eyes
apocalyptic visions had spun their
incessant details until a
   kind of glossolalia had
taken over,
now spoke with crystalline clarity.

Then the King of Locusts called everyone to
   attention. He said with utmost

simplicity and decorum: "Although we may be
    impatient for a showdown,
and fed up with mankind in all its
manifestations, we are still under
    command here, and can do
        nothing without
            divine go-ahead."

Rivers of Pus shimmered. Plague of Frogs
shifted uneasily, licking a billion
flies out of the air in an eyeblink.

The Sun Like a Ball of Blood rose and
proclaimed itself slave to Allah like
everything else,

and for one more day the plowman
plowed his golden wheat,

the murderer murdered without
    compunction,

the corrupt politician dreamed of
yachts in the Caribbean, and the

saintly mother tucked her children
    in with a kiss.

                                                8/23

EYELASH

If our whole universe is just an eyelash
   floating in the Real World,
all our wars and bloodshed,
grief and wringing of hands and
heaviness of heart
as well as
all the majestic canyons and geysers of this
   frosted and fuzzy planet and
all far planets and galaxies in which
   we are just one bubble-blink
one hiccup of time's worth
     in one blip of space —

all the farthest reaches of our universe
shaped in whatever shape, with whatever clearly
delineated limits it may have, S shaped or a
doughnut shape pulled monstrously
through itself inside-out, or a
   long floaty arm
crook'd but relaxed through infinite
   leeway —

if all this itself in God's Eye is only an
eyelash afloat in Reality, and we will
wake to it one day after the angel has
   taken the trumpet mouthpiece
     down from its blue translucent
         lips,

and all the floating debris of
former and present worlds
has come to a sudden halt,
and all of space has become an ear
listening to God's featheriest breathing,

then we will show the light of our faces
surrounded by silver rainbows of indescribable
    splendor,

and in our own eyes the eyelash irritant that
  woke us in the first place
will be plucked out by one stroke of angelic deftness

and we will see the irritant as the
machine of illumination that it is,

and we will say, *"Our Lord,*
you fill all space
    with Your light!"

                                                                             8/24

THE BEE

The bee as it stings and dies sings a
   song of farewell as it realizes,
heard at a sub-molecular level
by the inflamed lump it leaves on the
   flank of its last lover:
      Death.

The trumpet note,
after it's sounded, enters an
  arc of disappearing waves,
white sheets of silence folding after it
   until it is gone. Only
quiet remains.

The building is so silent, crumbling
   to dust. We enter and
climb its stairs, papers
floating in the air. The building slowly
   becomes:
      nowhere.

Things of space and time, like
soundless animals of light, endangered species
entering extinction with a smile,
leave their ghostly signatures on the
  air, signed with a slow flourish,
uncharacteristically clear.

We look through eyes that will one day
   blankly stare.
At a disappeared world that will
materially
   still be here.

But that which sees
   the things we look at
will then be
    elsewhere.

That which sees is
the seeing of God

manifest in thin air.

                                                            8/28

LIGHT

Suddenly he couldn't turn the light off.

The switch was useless. *Click-click* all he
liked, the light stayed on.

The room became incandescent.
It seemed as if walls and floor
   had simply melted.

There he was with a predicament. He
   couldn't turn the light off at the switch
and he couldn't reach the light itself to
smash or otherwise demolish it.

Someone came upon him, saw the situation and
went away. Then two people came.
After a while more and more people came.

He was beginning to almost see things.
Herds of crystal bison moving at an alarming
   rate through what used to be the
     walls. Rivers of shards of brilliance
silently cascading through space.

And the light only seemed to be getting
   brighter and brighter.

He began to feel himself kind of

melting into its superior element.

Crowds gathered, hushed groups and
   ecstatic individuals. They felt
healed. He had no power to
   hurt or heal, but due to his
connection with this phenomenon
he found himself capable of
     unusual things.

He spoke with unaccustomed brevity and
   eloquence.
Where he would go on and on with a kind of
well-meaning enthusiasm, driving his
  points home with inspired bits of
    intensely punctuated detail,
now he left things hanging in the air
unconcluded, but all the more
     pungent.

Heads of state came, but he felt no
special awe. Religious leaders came
and he always felt great deferential
respect and love for their
  titanic efforts to understand and
realize the truth in their
    lifetimes.

He actually wept at people he felt
had failed to make it to the goal,
who had squandered themselves, or simply

fell back in exhaustion before the
   ultimate effortless effort
      had been made.

The light became more intense. The room seemed to
   grow wider beyond all
      expectations.

People he had known no longer actually
   recognized him. He seemed to have
      changed that much.

But it was simply
where he left off and
where the light began
had disappeared.

                                            8/31

CRICKET

The cricket at my door all night
  sings insistently that sweet irregular
mechanical whistle crickets sing
in the black night

which I hear with my human ears,
but in the cricket world of armored
green-plated body, huge dome eyes, feelers,
back legs rubbing their musical hairs,
what is it crickets perceive in such
nighttime racket? Pure

music? Schubert-rich textures in
  wet grass. Longing? Joy? Is this
language, somewhere between the
still chorales of stones and
world treaties between nations?

Is this treaties between cricket nations?

Between total silence and the coming sounds of day?

Is he singing: *"Woe is me, a*
  lowly cricket! Even I
    perceive my God!" Does he

know or care that others listen, that
I sit on bed-edge writing this

insect meditation, my own transparent
   veined wings trembling? My own
mandibles clenched. My own song

determined by who I am: *"Woe is me,
a lowly man. Not quite so clear.*

I long for God. And me to

   disappear!"

                                                  9/4

WATER RUNNING IN THE PIPES

Water running in the pipes in the house announces
   somebody's awake at 5:30 A.M. moving
     in their own space of consciousness,
just as the high-pitched mosquito who just
   buzzed into my right ear, but I missed,
just as the two other people in our family
assuredly still snoozing, eye movements and
   breathing rhythms indicating which
celestial transport to technicolor binauralism or
   blank deep sleep of just guttural whispers,
the two cats also, their paws and tails
arranged for comfort, or cavorting
   noisily as they often do at this angelic
     hour, bouncing up or down the
stairs or sliding across the throw rugs
(we find them in the morning scrunched and
   rumpled),
and then multiply this hasty inventory by the
millions or even billions to get some idea of
the lively glitter of this round planet beyond
  (and because of) its solar reflection,
to know in our bones within its intricate fabric
the uninventible miracle of life God's
breathed into the whole creation any moment
one pretends to stop for a minute (which
   can't be done), to cock an ear or
take a look at it, its
    irrepressible song.

                                            9/5

ALL YOUR MESSAGES

1

All your messages are messages of farewell
and all my messages are messages of longing.

I arrive at the train station and the
   train is pulling away until
     only steam fills my view with darker
swirls inside spelling out *"separation."*

I walk down a street near an open window and can
almost identify the tune you are humming
and the window slides down.

Oh, how long can it go on like this, my
   always just missing meeting you?

When roses are about to bloom
I'm taken to live in another city where
   the bushes are sere and brown.

Friends tell me of the skylark's dive in
   open fields day after day, but when I go
rain is falling, night is falling,
leaves are falling from the trees,
and my heart is falling slowly as an elevator
past floors I long to stop at, down and
   down interminably and silently

through a whispering shaft of light and darkness.

Will it arrive at its destination, a
   glowing sunlit meadow with meandering
     stream by white blossoms?

And will you greet me there?

And after we meet will all my longing be
   fulfilled, and will your space
I long to disappear in always afford me
the sweetness our hearts desire? Will
windows open in it, and will the
   steam-billowing transport
on parallel rails take me to the
     true source of light?

2

All your messages are messages of "perhaps,"
and all my messages are out-and-out pleas.

The tent flap hangs across the doorway, and
   in the dust-haze I see a rider
     retreating or arriving, but the
   heat is so intense and the air is
     thick with longing.

Even I am not sure if I arrive or
   depart.

*"The trail to where we are has many loops.
The trail away from here is straight."*

I've seen the moon hang on the branch of the
   sky with such swollen fever it
     looked like it might
    drop off onto earth and go out.

The night would be lost without you, even if
you never show yourself.

Men and women who live on rumors
   would grow afraid of the silence,
while those who navigate by your light
would have to learn the map of the stars.

The wind carries your name.

The wind touches my fingertips like
   Braille to a blind man
spelling your name on my senses —

*At least
I have that to go by.*

                                             9/7-11

SOME SLEEP!

Some sleep! I wake up and
   Lucretia Borgia's mixing nasty
tinctures by my head!

Some sleep! I wake up and innocent
Iraqi civilians
  lie dead in a wheel around me.
Babies lie on stomachs of mothers
    equally dead.

Some sleep! I wake up and
   American politicians mouth
sweet nothings into my ear.
I wake up and the world has changed
color and texture and sound.
Yesterday birds gathered at
   dusk and car horns and sirens blew —
now it's the crashing of giant waves of
   fiery asphalt and distant
      winds.

Some sleep! I
wake up out of sound sleep
and the world's become
     transparent.
Where genteel folk in form-fitting clothes
roamed at will and made thoughtful decisions
now I see wild beasts yowling and

   gnashing sharp teeth.
Pterodactyls sail in a deep purple sky.
Dinosaurs thunder. Prehistoric
   reality is as poignant as
the reality of now

only its footprints are bigger.

Some sleep! I
  wake up and
things are suddenly the
same as they always were.
Sharper-edged but full of
the same light. Shorter, but casting
the same long shadows.

I go back to sleep.

                                                    9/14

THE EAR THAT HEARS IT

for Karen Markham

You speak of your symphony as being as
   wide as the desert or as
     wide as the sky above the desert,
and of nothing happening,

of waves of energy pouring into space
or the space of the desert or the
   space of the sky above the desert
and of nothing happening.

You speak of the whole piece stopping to go
   down into prostration as if by itself
and yet nothing is happening,

a stone or two casting shadow on the
hard desert sand, a
   twig or tendril of vegetation or two
    also casting faint spidery shadow
on the flat desert surface going in
all directions for miles at once
and the sky originating anywhere you begin
in space above the desert surface

spreading or flattening out in four dimensions,
for time is involved though you said it is
timeless and that

nothing happens, no movement, a
    tone somewhere deep in the heart of
        the something where nothing happens,

a throb like the depths of the ocean or the
origin of space in deep space that
pulsates in a place where
nothing happens,

yet it is hard to imagine, hard to hear
sound that has no duration or
duration that is soundless, hard to
imagine a sensation while not
    actually being there to be
        overwhelmed by its
pulse or else overwhelmed by its
    silence,

to be, in all this,
the ear that hears it,
the ear like all this,

an exact replica of the
stretching sand and sky,

that actually hears it.

                                                     9/15

FUNERAL PRACTICES

Some bury their dead on tall wooden platforms of
   birch boughs lashed together
and thongs tie the body wrapped in
   blankets and ritual cloaks and the
elements draw its constituent parts
back into themselves bit by bit until
wind howls through skeletal
   structures of platform and bones, the
soul released into non-structures of light and
totally free.

Some carry their dead to plateaus on
rocky Himalayan heights and chop the bodies up to make them
easy for vultures to devour,
returning after a year to grind the remains into
even more easily edible powder. Wind blows the
   last bits free.

Some bury their dead in ivory mausoleums on
   desert sands far away from cities
so only the sun and moon
slide light over their contours, or
   the occasional pilgrim awed suddenly
by the sweet-smelling
     palpable emptiness.

Some bury their dead in ornate coffins with
cushions, sashes and hinges of
gold, and they're lowered like the

Titanic into walled-in holes
   made ready for such
royalty, sealed like a tomb awaiting
the next phase, whatever it might be.

Some bury their dead in pewter urns set on
shelves among family jars or
alone on a mantelpiece in a house
   frequented only in summer, the
ashes inside
settling quietly into silence, the grandchildren
wide-eyed whenever they compare the
musty photograph of happy grandpa on the porch
with the sealed vase on the mantelpiece
gathering late summer dust.

Some bury their dead in a fiery pyre of
aromatic spices and wood, or in a
mythical beast created from balsa
   that burns both
its body and the human body inside as orange flames
   consume form to release
The Formless into sparks and floating
     ash
in the wide cemetery of the air —
and what remains of the body is ash mixed with
   balsa and spice, wind fiddling with
all the elements in its path and
     flinging them aside.

Some bury their dead by placing them

lovingly in canoes filled with
    pine boughs, amulets and
   beads, thong-lashed and
eyeless the dead head out across calm waters
from bay to sea and
    from sea to sky.

Some bury their dead fastidiously, rouging their
cheeks, buffing their fingernails, combing
    their hair,

others pile the dead
on top of each other, face down, arms and legs
   akimbo, hundreds to a grave they
bulldoze in hopes
grass will grow quickly
so it will never be found.

Others bury their dead after dessicating the
  body and using the skeleton as a
    strut for sculpture, decorating the
skull with inlaid mother-of-pearl and
turquoise, the glittering figures finally sitting
together in ancestral pantheons.

Some bury their dead washed and
camphor-rubbed, wrapped in
sweet-smelling cloth, faces exposed,
laid on their sides in the ground so they can
open their spiritual eyes
    and contemplate Paradise.

Some bury their dead by drifting their
cremated ashes from hovering helicopters into the
San Francisco Bay, leaving mourners on shore.

But the living go on, eyes fastened on heaven,
feet heavily shod, days and
   nights passing with a nearly
     weightless physicality

from birth-canal to high school cubbyhole to
hotel bedroom to grave in the side of a hill

in late afternoon sunlight

soon bathed in moonlight

by midnight.

                                                            9/18

RAIN

I suppose I could realistically describe the
rain pelting down straight down onto the
streets as I drive my daughter's friends home
in the night, water reflecting off the
wet blackboards of the streets and the
pulsing curtain of rain like crystal
beads glittering in a constant movie of
motion and water splashing the
windshield the windshield wipers part like
the Red Sea waters pushed aside left and right to let
Moses and the Children of Israel through

in my momentary jealousy of the Poetry Festival
poets who stood in equally momentary glory at
glittering microphones with their prizes and
publications and read approbrious thoughtful
poems rarely daring the impossible or
venturing into realms of the Unseen and
so careful about their references to God or
His influence or radiance, some
even denouncing the very idea as tyrannical
and oppressive,
others coyly admitting the possibility, one or
two bravely but metaphorically announcing
God's Presence, but none, not one theist or
atheist able to forget God for long
either positively or negatively
in our climate of cultural skepticism and

utter awe before science as well as the
science of personality, its successes and failures,
but none entering pure drunkenness,

and I could mention the sound of water
cascading all around us, hitting the car roof
with its aqueous staccato, or back

home as I write this, safe and dry, the rain
abating, pervasive gurgles and drips of it
stereophonically surrounding us,

and the great rains of the past, the floods and
terrestrial inundations,
waves out of control, overflowing the
  margins and boundaries, whole persons
drowned, arms and faces above water,

or the drops themselves, each separate, each
incandescent with angelic excitement,
plummeting to earth, earthwardly
   commanded, mercy direct to our
need in this world's miraculous
  elemental balance, wet and
dry cunningly alternating, fall now
   insisting on eradicating summer,
green things beaten to the ground, pummelled
  by glorious drops, hammered into
submission, as we are
by our mortality, earthworms happy to be
   moistened, the drops each a

palace of moisture, gathering into
pools at their destinations, or
furiously coursing as rivers, or the

most mysteriously beautiful
   vision of all, of rampaging
  storms at sea, sky and sea
    utterly mingling, ships going
down with all hands,
the sky a confabulation of wings, of
  Spirit charging in sheets across
    the landscape, of
black streaks of wet in the blackness,

the whole house I'm in now rising,
lifted on a giant wave,
relaxed at the peak then slid
  down into a trough, yet
stillness pervading, no motion at
    all except in my heart's brain,

I see processions of rain-streaks with
faces coming forward, each wet hand
  raised in compassion, each
mouth forming words unspoken,
watery faces filling heaven. God's

  Voice in the rain all around us.

9/29

BIG BOAT OF THE NIGHT

The big boat of the night has left me on the
   shore of the jujubees, gelatinous
savages, werewolves who don't even need
the lunar assistance of a full moon to turn
beastly.

Grass itself grows on wire strands,
Birds are all mechanical,
Sky has been painted black.

I'm well received by the natives who don't get
   much company,
they go around stark naked, except that for them
such exposure only hides them further,
their bodies covered with a cross between
   scales and fur.

I'm invited to tea by a grande dame of high
   society, little open-faced
     sandwiches and petit-fours,
   fizzy things in tall glasses.
We look out her window onto a silver lake.

I can't seem to begin this poem and I
   can't seem to stop it.

Have mercy on me, O Lord. Have mercy.

                                                    9/30

THE SOUL

The soul is a green river snaking through
    gray territory.
White kites fly above in a blue sky.
Larvae the size of statuary
  sing anthems of their domains
    without sound.
Scientifically precise descriptions of the tiny
   hairs on the inside and outside of things
curled or straight, springy or flat, long or
    short, are accompanied by
enlarged color photos that include some of the
   areas surrounding, which resemble
maps of China or San Diego.

But in spite of all this minutia
the soul is a green river snaking through
    gray territory
as if on an outing in the country of all things
large and small as they are
  haphazardly arranged against the
    bright green of a hillside.

Green river, green hillside: thus the soul's
   consubstantiality with all things, else
how could we know the longing "moo" of the calf
    for her ma, or the squirrel's
chattery anger as he hangs half down from a
branch scolding me for

surprising him nibbling the trash?
How could we know the ants' intrepid industry
and somehow empathize with all its
   non-wheezing and stoic lack of attitude while
carrying impossible things up walls?

The soul flies like a magic bird between trees,
its crystalline wingspread like two silver
   seas extending their surf line to the
absolute edges of sense.

The soul is beyond sense. Beyond time or
stillness or flight. It sits at the
bottom of a lake and converses with fish,
it floats between galaxies communicating with
orbits, it slides down the throat of the
lover fulfilled after nearly
jumping out a mouth into thin air
propelled by the heart in total love with its
own annihilation into what is

greater than it in the

cosmic scheme of things.

                                            10/4

STRAIGHT ON AHEAD THROUGH GREEN

At any one moment,
the burns, cuts, nicks, scratches, chigger-bites,
    skin abrasions, blisters, bunions, any
of these inflicted imperfections on our bodies,
are battle scars of the spirit's encounter with matter,
of our bodies at the front lines of worldly reality,

a burn on the left wrist from colliding even
    briefly with the hot brass floor lamp top,
mysterious bite soreness and redness that
    took place in the night while sleeping
from mosquito or flea or some other hungry
        marauder,
small paper cut at left thumb while
    inadvertently leafing through
        furniture catalog way out of
            price range in the first place,
bump on ankle from clonking against
    metal pole sticking halfway out the
        ground,
red sore bridge of nose from colliding
    briefly with cabinet door pressing
glasses' nose piece against aforesaid bridge of nose,
    some strange bite or eruption on
        top of head, either from outside
nasty encounter with something sharp and hard
or from inside volcanic
    eruption, thought or synapse,

then there's all the
inside invasions our precious, overworked and
underpaid immune system attacks, made
   famous by recent PR with AIDS,
unseen globular battles where cells attack
  enemies and absorb them neatly into their
own luminous bodies to
   neutralize them,
strange whipping two-headed beasties microscopically
large but potentially lethal at any one moment
eyeing the liver or pancreas or some choice
  arterial cluster or other,

all these encroachments outside or inside us
the visceral battle map with X's and flags
of our earth-wandering as we go from
bundle of babyness to bundle at
   death,

the soul's pure journey encased in its
battered physical vehicle,
  stopping for red lights,
slowing for yellow, careening with full force
  straight on ahead through
      green.

                                                10/5

NOTEBOOK

1

As he writes in his notebook the notebook
   falls apart.
As he lets his pen glide across horizons of beautifully
    level blue lines
the pages detach themselves from the binding and
     turn to dust.

Not just any old dust.
But dust with sunbeams plunging into it
   as if from a very high barn window,
golden laterals slanting down into a dark interior and
disappearing into the dust from the
pages that have turned to dust as
    fast as he writes on them.

The words themselves then decompose as he
composes, wriggle back into themselves, the
black and loopy circular lines of his
handwriting, like some magic spray-can from a
   novelty store, suck back into their
point of origin as fast as he forms
letters into words, cutting with the black
string of his writing into the general
   snow-covered hillsides of the
blank pages of his disappearing notebook as he writes.

If he snorts, or sniffs or mouths the
    words as he writes
an eraser of silence sweeps across and
      silences him.

The longer he writes, the more words he
   covers blank pages with,
the more empty the space of his perceptions,
the more concave the convex world becomes,
until the fiery trees and majestic
    dragonflies of his vision
become white wisps of dust coiling in
      front of a white wall,

and silence engulfs him and his
entire enterprise.

2

But is it the death knell, or is it
   signs of life that this

simultaneous appearance and
disappearance should take place?

As the crystal fountain opens out and
    begins to operate, images
     being displayed in graceful spray
       that does not wet or splash,

at the same moment palaces, once domains of
    rajahs, now five-star hotels,
disappear brick by intricately carved brick
into the steaming cauldrons of their foundations,
and animate beings,
  as soon as they blink their eyes
  open, blink their whole selves
    closed and are
gone simultaneously with coming into being,

no echo hanging in air after them, with only the
    most fragile of afterimages,

while he most diligently
writes and writes in his notebook.

3

The cat spent five minutes sitting still on the table top
staring straight into my face, with
  affection? Some mystically driven
X-ray intensity? Predatory hunger? I'll
  never truly know, except that,
although purring mightily, she
  twisted away when I put her on her
    back in my arms and
      scratched her belly, only
briefly putting her head back and
  submitting, almost smilingly.

I could call out troops and invade
Mongolia, I could
   outfit ships and discover
      Anarctica,

but instead I write forward in my notebook
not knowing where it will lead,
forward out of blankness, words forming
   electrical landscapes of
      possibility, where a
tunnel might suddenly appear full of
   deep purple light rays, and out of

their shower a white tiger strides and
looks straight into my face with
cat-sharp eyes of an exotic
   beauty only
Baudelaire comes close to with his
sumptuous mulatta mistress, her

tinkling brass hoop earrings, her
slant eyes and
small brown breasts.

                                    10/8-10

PASSING A CRUSHED SQUIRREL ON THE HIGHWAY

I think of your family

but they're probably not thinking of you,

if *"thinking"* is the proper word to use

for what squirrels do.

OCEAN

I wonder what it would be like to
    hear the ocean crashing nearby
out our window in Philadelphia
    miles away from any actual shore,

the rhythmic *shhhhhh* sound crashing and
    receding constantly, as I
thought I almost heard it in my
head a moment ago, and remembered

living near the ocean once in California, or
staying at a friend's house in San Francisco overnight
where I could hear the amazing sound of
ocean from anywhere in the house, as if

the waters were reaching underneath it and
splattering among rocks, sizzling underneath us and
pulling back again far out to sea
under a yellow moon, in yellow moonlight,

thrashing in undulous waves and bubbling froth
in a vast expanse that becomes the
entire horizon, blank as slate but
tumultuous as a basket of snakes,

water all around us, water in
our bodies and in the sky and air

circulating and circulating around us
calling out God's Name in articulate
syllables of water, wherever there is
water, in Rangoon and Timor, canals and
rivers through rainforest and
   shantytown, watery

   eloquence!

But here in the city, by sound of refrigerator or
steam heat or passing car,
there's no ocean around us, except
   conceptually, whereas

outside this window could be the
calliope crashing of ocean sound that is actually
   way inside our heads but whose

shore is deeper in space and farther into
the astral light of things than we think.

                                               10/16

WHAT HE'LL HAVE TO LEARN

He'll have to learn the ways of the inclined plane,
of right angles and gravity, of how
   light travels from a tip to a tip, from
     match to candle-wick.

He'll have to learn rotations and accelerations,
  shapes and precise locations unknown
    even to the people who inhabit them
who're in the habit of calling their few
    thousand acres "The World."

He'll have to put his strange feet with their
  flexible flesh-colored
    toes and hard nails on the ends
as flat as possible on the
earth and try to keep from falling off,
keeping his balance precariously by learning
simple alphabets with complicated
  pronunciations, aspirated "h's",
silent "c's", looping melodic
  rises and falls, as well as
    pregnant silences.

He'll have to learn about his eyes and how to use them,
rolling them to emphasize a point or
  communicate doubt about a speaker's
veracity. He'll have to learn when to make
  eye contact and when to

avoid it, when to use
words carefully chosen and when to
keep silent. He'll have to
    learn these things.

Then when he's learned all these things and is
safely enclosed in them as if again in the
womb, he'll have to

unlearn them all, let them
blow completely away, let
light pry under all their edges to
    invade them,

plummeting to the essences of all these special
  knowledges, releasing the trapdoors of
deep inner meanings, such as the
deep inner meaning of the inclined plane and the
radiant innermost meaning of gravity which is
   angelic laughter and invisible beings in a
      stone, grim
protector demons
of a wall, sudden divine permission
of a door,

and he'll tumble into space like a
downy feather twisting this way and
that on his lighter-than-air journey to
the Creator of Light, the Creator of Air,

Whose puff of breath is what we

live on, His skillfully rippling and
    branching air-currents

keeping us
afloat.

                                        10/16

INDEX

A New Stone 113
A Version of Petrarch 109
Advice in our Sleep 133
All Your Messages 203
Angels Sing 82
Answered Prayer 118
At the Command of the Sky 68
Baby Dawn Blue 123
Behind Every Patch of Sunlight 137
Big Boat of the Night 217
Blizzard Bacchanal 66
Cat 64
Configurations of Sleepers 42
Contemplation on the Rocks 101
Cricket 200
Dawn Prayer 62
Dawn Song 116
Drunken Aphorisms 16
Ember Falling Through Space 69
Everything Was as it Should Be 176
Eyelash 193
Fables Written During a Flight from Chicago to Philadelphia 180
First One Angel 121
First-hand Sunlight, First-hand Rock 105
From Where I Sit 155
Funeral Practices 210
God's Echo 32
God's in the Details 76
Greenness of My Garden 162
Hands to the Sides of our Heads 89
I Don't Know 158

I End My Song   169
I Look Through My Eyes   23
I Scent My Beard Before I Sleep   20
I Spy a Land Beyond Clouds   149
I Wake up With a Start   188
In the Courtyard of the Prophets   30
In the Tiniest Mirror   53
In This World of Multiple Solitaries   160
It's a Different Location   59
It's Hard if You're Dead   165
Journey   84
Keeping Watch   174
King of Locusts   191
Light   197
Little Black Fly on the Wall   156
Maybe Nobody's Really Happy   97
Microscopic Twigs   25
Mind Piano   72
Mother Tongue   146
Multi-Colored Skies   36
Nature Poetry   95
New York   186
Notebook   222
Nude, I Bear You   87
Ocean   227
On This Side of Sleep   128
One of Us   151
Orchestrated by Angels   55
Other-Dimensional Latitudes   28
Out in the Longitudinal Air   163
Passing a Crushed Squirrel on the Highway   226
Possible Angels   131
Put Ladders Up Against the Sky Everywhere   13

Pythian the Angler   189
Rain   214
Reply to a Letter from a Long-Lost Friend   50
Résumé   141
Returning from a Marvelous Journey   11
Ruby Red   134
Shadow on the Moon   47
Snail   34
Some Sleep!   206
Song for the Millennium   153
Stethoscope   43
Straight on Ahead Through Green   220
Sunflower of Fortune   38
The Alchemist's Lapse   124
The Bee   195
The Ear That Hears It   208
The Rain Has Been Falling   184
The Sky is Red   58
The Soul   218
The Treasury of the Sky   19
The Well   45
The World   86
Tom-Tom   171
Trees, For All Their Beauty   110
Upward Shower of Pure Sound   178
Watching People Pass By   79
Water Running in the Pipes   202
We Have Come a Long Way   107
What He'll Have to Learn   229
When Someone   100
Wrong Side of the Bed   114

ABOUT THE AUTHOR

Born in 1940 in Oakland, California, Daniel Abdal-Hayy Moore had his first book of poems, *Dawn Visions*, published by Lawrence Ferlinghetti of City Lights Books, San Francisco, in 1964, and the second in 1972, *Burnt Heart/Ode to the War Dead*. He created and directed *The Floating Lotus Magic Opera Company* in Berkeley, California in the late 60s, and presented two major productions, *The Walls Are Running Blood*, and *Bliss Apocalypse*. He became a Sufi Muslim in 1970, performed the Hajj in 1972, and lived and traveled throughout Morocco, Spain, Algeria and Nigeria, landing in California and publishing *The Desert is the Only Way Out*, and *Chronicles of Akhira* in the early 80s (Zilzal Press). Residing in Philadelphia since 1990, in 1996 he published *The Ramadan Sonnets* (Jusoor/City Lights), and in 2002, *The Blind Beekeeper* (Jusoor/Syracuse University Press). He has been the major editor for a number of works, including *The Burdah* of Shaykh Busiri, translated by Hamza Yusuf, and the poetry of Palestinian poet, Mahmoud Darwish, translated by Munir Akash. He is also widely published on the worldwide web: *The American Muslim*, *DeenPort*, and his own website and poetry blog, among others: *www.danielmoorepoetry.com*, *www.ecstaticxchange.wordpress.com*. He has been poetry editor for *Seasons Journal*, *Islamica Magazine*, a 2010 translation by Munir Akash of *State of Siege*, by Mahmoud Darwish (Syracuse University Press), and *The Prayer of the Oppressed*, by Imam Muhammad Nasir al-Dar'i, translated by Hamza Yusuf. In 2011 and 2012 he was a winner of the Nazim Hikmet Prize for Poetry. In 2013 he won an American Book Award, and was listed among The 500 Most Influential Muslims for 2013, for his poetry. *The Ecstatic Exchange Series* is bringing out the extensive body of his works of poetry (a complete list of published works on page 2).

POETIC WORKS by Daniel Abdal-Hayy Moore
Published and Unpublished

Dawn Visions (published by City Lights, 1964)
Burnt Heart/Ode to the War Dead (published by City Lights, 1972)
This Body of Black Light Gone Through the Diamond (printed by Fred Stone, Cambridge, Mass, 1965)
On The Streets at Night Alone (1965?)
All Hail the Surgical Lamp (1967)
States of Amazement (1970)

Abdallah Jones and the Disappearing-Dust Caper (published by The Ecstatic Exchange/Crescent Series, 2006)
'Ala ud-Deen and the Magic Lamp (published by The Ecstatic Exchange, 2011)
The Chronicles of Akhira (1981) (published by Zilzal Press with Typoglyphs by Karl Kempton, 1986; published in Sparrow on the Prophet's Tomb by The Ecstatic Exchange, 2009)
Mouloud (1984) (A Zilzal Press chapbook, 1995; published in Sparrow on the Prophet's Tomb by The Ecstatic Exchange, 2009)
The Crown of Creation (1984) (published by The Ecstatic Exchange, 2012)
The Look of the Lion (The Parabolas of Sight) (1984)
The Desert is the Only Way Out (completed 4/21/84) (Zilzal Press chapbook, 1985)
Atomic Dance (1984) (am here books, 1988)
Outlandish Tales (1984)
Awake as Never Before (12/26/84) (Zilzal Press chapbook, 1993)
Glorious Intervals (1/1/85) (Zilzal Press chapbook, ?)
Long Days on Earth/Book I (1/28 – 8/30/85)
Long Days on Earth/Book II (Hayy Ibn Yaqzan)
Long Days on Earth/Book III (1/22/86)
Long Days on Earth/Book IV (1986)
The Ramadan Sonnets (Long Days on Earth/Book V) (5/9 – 6/11/86) (published by Jusoor/City Lights Books, 1996) (republished as Ramadan Sonnets by The Ecstatic Exchange, 2005)
Long Days on Earth/Book VI (6-8/30/86)
Holograms (9/4/86 – 3/26/87)
History of the World (The Epic of Man's Survival) (4/7 – 6/18/87)
Exploratory Odes (6/25 – 10/18/87)

The Man at the End of the World (11/11 – 12/10/87)
The Perfect Orchestra (3/30 – 7/25/88)(published by The Ecstatic Exchange, 2009)
Fed from Underground Springs (7/30 – 11/23/88)
Ideas of the Heart (11/27/88 – 5/5/89)
New Poems (scattered poems, out of series, from 3/24 – 8/9/89)
Facing Mecca (5/16 – 11/11/89)
A Maddening Disregard for the Passage of Time (11/17/89 – 5/20/90) (published by The Ecstatic Exchange, 2009)
The Heart Falls in Love with Visions of Perfection (6/15/90 – 6/2/91)
Like When You Wave at a Train and the Train Hoots Back at You (Farid's Book) (6/11 – 7/26/91) (published by The Ecstatic Exchange, 2008)
Orpheus Meets Morpheus (8/1/91– 3/14/92)
The Puzzle (3/21/92 – 8/17/93)(published by The Ecstatic Exchange, 2011)
The Greater Vehicle (10/17/93 – 4/30/94)
A Hundred Little 3-D Pictures (5/14/94 – 9/11/95) (published by The Estatic Exchange, 2013)
The Angel Broadcast (9/29 – 12/17/95)
Mecca/Medina Time-Warp (12/19/95 – 1/6/96) (published as a Zilzal Press chapbook, 1996)(published in Sparrow on the Prophet's Tomb, 2009)
Miracle Songs for the Millennium (1/20 – 10/16/96)(published by The Ecstatic Exchange, 2014)
The Blind Beekeeper (11/15/96 – 5/30/97) (published 2002 by Jusoor/Syracuse University Press)
Chants for the Beauty Feast (6/3 – 10/28/97)(published by The Ecstatic Exchange, 2011
You Open a Door and it's a Starry Night (10/29/97 – 5/23/98) (published by The Ecstatic Exchange, 2009)
Salt Prayers (5/29 – 10/24/98) (published by The Ecstatic Exchange, 2005)
Some (10/25/98 – 4/25/99)
Flight to Egypt (5/1 – 5/16/99)
I Imagine a Lion (5/21 – 11/15/99) (published by The Ecstatic Exchange, 2006)
Millennial Prognostications (11/25/99 – 2/2/2000) (published by the Ecstatic Exchange, 2009)
Shaking the Quicksilver Pool (2/4 – 10/8/2000) (published by The Ecstatic Exchange, 2009)
Blood Songs (10/9/2000 – 4/3/2001)(Published by The Ecstatic Exchange, 2012)

The Music Space (4/10 – 9/16/2001) (published by The Ecstatic Exchange, 2007)

Where Death Goes (9/20/2001 – 5/1/2002) (published by The Ecstatic Exchange, 2009)

The Flame of Transformation Turns to Light (99 Ghazals Written in English) (5/14 – 8/21/2002) (published by The Ecstatic Exchange, 2007)

Through Rose-Colored Glasses (7/22/2002 – 1/15/2003) (published by The Ecstatic Exchange, 2007)

Psalms for the Broken-Hearted (1/22 – 5/25/2003) (published by The Ecstatic Exchange, 2006)

Hoopoe's Argument (5/27 – 9/18/03)

Love is a Letter Burning in a High Wind (9/21 – 11/6/2003) (published by The Ecstatic Exchange, 2006)

Laughing Buddha/Weeping Sufi (11/7/2003 – 1/10/2004) (published by The Ecstatic Exchange, 2005)

Mars and Beyond (1/20 – 3/29/2004) (published by The Ecstatic Exchange, 2005)

Underwater Galaxies (4/5 – 7/21/2004) (published by The Ecstatic Exchange, 2007)

Cooked Oranges (7/23/2004 – 1/24/2005 (published by The Ecstatic Exchange, 2007)

Holiday from the Perfect Crime (1/25 – 6/11/2005)(published by The Ecstatic Exchange, 2011)

Stories Too Fiery to Sing Too Watery to Whisper (6/13 – 10/24/2005)

Coattails of the Saint (10/26/2005 – 5/10/2006) (published by The Ecstatic Exchange, 2006)

In the Realm of Neither (5/14/2006 – 11/12/06) (published by The Ecstatic Exchange, 2008)

Invention of the Wheel (11/13/06 – 6/10/07)(published by The Ecstatic Exchange, 2010)

The Sound of Geese Over the House (6/15 – 11/4/07)

The Fire Eater's Lunchbreak (11/11/07 – 5/19/2008) (published by The Ecstatic Exchange, 2008)

Sparks Off the Main Strike (5/24/2008 – 1/10/2009)(published by The Ecstatic Exchange, 2010)

Stretched Out on Amethysts (1/13 – 9/17/2009)(published by The Ecstatic Exchange, 2010)

The Throne Perpendicular to All that is Horizontal (9/18/09 – 1/25/10)
In Constant Incandescence (2/10 – 8/13/10) (published by The Ecstatic
    Exchange, 2011)
The Caged Bear Spies the Angel (8/30/10 – 3/6/11)(published by The Ecstatic
    Exchange, 2010)
This Light Slants Upward (3/7 – 10/13/11)
Ramadan is Burnished Sunlight (part of This Light Slants Upward,
    published separately by The Ecstatic Exchange, 2011)
The Match That Becomes a Conflagration (10/14/11 – 5/9/12)
Down at the Deep End (5/10 – 8/3/12) (published by The Ecstatic
    Exchange, 2012)
Next Life (8/9/12 – 2/12/13) (published by The Ecstatic Exchange, 2013)
The Soul's Home (2/13 – 10/8/13)
Eternity Shimmers & Time Holds its Breath (10/10/13 – 1/27/14)
He Comes Running (part of Eternity Shimmers, published as an Ecstatic
    Exchange Chapbook, 2014)
The Sweet Enigma of it All (1/28/14 –)

www.ingramcontent.com/pod-product-compliance
Lightning Source LLC
Chambersburg PA
CBHW022057160426
43198CB00008B/266